UNDER
—*the*—
SHELTER
ALONE WITH GOD, LEARNING TO TRUST HIM

Mary Swift Kelly

WESTBOW
PRESS®
A DIVISION OF THOMAS NELSON
& ZONDERVAN

To my loving husband, Dick

and

My sons

Robert
Joseph
Jonathan
Richard

CONTENTS

ACKNOWLEDGMENTS

I publically want to thank and bless these wonderful people,
not only for what they have done for me but most especially
for what they have done in the kingdom of God.
Well done, good and faithful servants.

To my husband, Dick, who has never held me back but has
given me the freedom to respond to God's calling on my life.

To my sons, Robert, Joseph, Jonathan, and Richard, great men
of God, who have spoken scripture and words of encouragement
to me when my heart was heavy and life seemed hopeless.

To my dear friend and spiritual mother, Gloria Evans, for helping me
with the conceptual configuration of this book, and my dear sister-in-
law Cindy Larsson and my husband Dick, for helping me with editing.

To my Monday night prayer group who have been faithfully
praying for over eighteen years for the needs of others and our
city, state, and nation. You have been called by God and
willingly have answered.

To Pastor Susan Omanson, who was a source of great
encouragement and friendship throughout all of my
First Baptist years and since. My sister in Christ.

To my friend and prayer partner, Sally Rice, who has been there
through the good and bad, praying, and whose friendship I cherish.

To Pastor Glenny Klumper, my accountability partner,
who has been a steadfast friend who has walked
with me through some of the darkest days.

To Pastor Bob Frickholm, who asked me to begin and
lead the prayer ministry at First Baptist Church, Sioux
Falls, South Dakota, and to its prayer ministers, whose
devotion to the Lord and love for people I cherish.

To Ted Hahs and Ed Silvoso, who believed in my calling and
whose support has blessed me. For their willingness to come
to Sioux Falls to teach on Marketplace Ministry and
City Transformation.

To Mike, Angie, Dede, and Pat for sharing
their lives with me and accepting
me into their family

To the many people who have invited me to
teach and speak in their churches
and at their conferences.

INTRODUCTION

Many people who hear me speak have told me that I need to write down my stories, so I begin with this book. The first two chapters give some background into my story and vision. The meditational devotions, prayers and insights in the subsequent chapters all have come as a result of the word and vision God spoke to me in 2003.

I got into the habit of journaling so I could remember the thoughts and revelations God was showing me. During my life I have walked through some very dark valleys and found writing helped. I not only wrote but found other creative hobbies like knitting, needlepoint, glass-painting, and stained glass to be most helpful as well; they all helped me to focus on the positive rather than on the negative.

The Bible says we all have been made in God's image. The image best recognized in me is definitely creativity. I must be creating something at all times, or I go crazy. Whether I am creating a home for a client, preparing a meal, painting, writing down an inspired morning thought, or writing this book, creating something beautiful is in my DNA.

A few years back, my husband, Dick, and I found an old, dilapidated farmhouse, which any normal person would have torn down and burned, but not me. I saw what it could be. With a lot of hard work and with the help of all eight of our kids, it has become our own little garden of Eden. I do the same with people. Too many people are like that old farmhouse, however, like that farmhouse, I can see what they could become, if loved and cared for.

The devotional thoughts found in this book are from my personal meditations. I have been journaling for years; this is a collection of my quiet-time moments while alone with God. Life is so full, and sitting quietly, waiting upon God to speak, is my favorite thing to do, especially at the beginning to the day. In fact, some mornings, when the weather and my bones permit, I love to take my coffee and go on a neighborhood walk with Jesus. I share everything with Him, blessing homes I pass and praying for those who come to mind.

I have been hungry for the Word since I became a believer in 1975. I love reading and studying the Bible because God speaks to me through His entire Word. There are places in the Bible where it says *selah*, which means to pause and think about the statement just read. I have used the word *selah* several times within my writings, and it is my hope that you will pause and meditate about the questions or statements, and let the Holy Spirit speak to you.

PREFACE

A Book of Remembrances—Memories of Lessons Learned

The scriptures have long been called God's love letter to us, but within the pages of this book is another love letter—one from a mother to her children. God wrote His love letter and so did I. These journal entries were selected from my collection of personal devotions with God. Talking with the Lord and journaling the things He shows me, is so precious to me! Two years ago, after a major surgery, I found myself in bed for six weeks. I had decided before the surgery, to organize all my writings and what I thought would be a six-week organizing of devotions turned out to be a two-year book. When I first read what I had written years ago, I soon realized how much deeper the Lord has taken me. Each one of the messages needed to be elaborated upon and fine-tuned.

Journaling helps me keep my focus on the truth and on Jesus. I want to share with you some of my thoughts and sacred quite times with God, and pray you will find value within these pages, that help guide and encourage you on your journey.

Throughout my life, I have learned from my experiences, some lessons were definitely more difficult than others, but all have opened my eyes to see God. Because Jesus loves us so, He wants us all to have an abundant life and to be safe, so stay away from the evil lurking in the world, it will destroy your life and your destiny. God's ways are not our ways, so learn how to trust Him and how to trust His Word. Stay under His loving protective shelter, and embrace the concepts within these pages. They may be difficult, but they will lead you toward the salvation of your soul and victory over the evil you will encounter. Always remember, "In this world you will have trouble. But take heart! I have overcome the world", (John 16:33) so, be strong and courageous, and be an overcomer!

Jesus once told me when I was first saved, "Your mom and dad love you and don't want to leave you, but someday they will, and it will be just you and Me. Your children love you and don't want to leave you, but someday they will grow up and leave, and it will be just you and Me. Your husband loves you and does not want to leave you, but someday he will, and it will be just you and Me." Just the Lord and me, walking together through life. So too for you. Your relationship with Jesus matters. Let Him confirm His awesome faithfulness to you and never trust your natural instincts. God alone is the one in whom you trust, so stay centered upon Christ and don't chase rabbit trails. It is all about Jesus.

To my children, I will love you forever and always, but Jesus loves you more, and it is His Holy Spirit who will help you and teach you. Lean upon Him. He is alive and He is faithful! I will not always be there for you, but Jesus will never leave you or forsake you. Let Him be your rock, the one you trust. And as Paul so perfectly says, "And I will make every effort to see that after my departure you will always be able to remember these things" (2 Peter 1:15 NIV).

Chapter 1

MARY'S STORY

I have often said I lost my mother at twelve. My older brother, Richard, along with two other high-school friends, were asphyxiated in a tragic accident. This one horrible moment in time completely changed the course of my life. Mother, lost in grief, seemed to disconnect from us, and to my childish mind, it seemed as if my sister, Beverly, Dad, and I no longer mattered. There were no grief clinics or therapy classes where Mom could get help. Prescription drugs gave her the relief she desperately needed for the pain. Days became weeks, then months, and then years. Mom fell prey to prescription drugs. It seemed like her only joy came from my little brother, Robert. Her whole world revolved around him, so for all practical purposes, I lost my older brother that day, but, sadly enough, I lost my mother as well.

Looking back, there have been so many chapters in my life, and it seems each chapter has taught me new lessons, each based on real-life experiences. The Bible says Christ identifies with us in all our sufferings and sorrows. When I think about my journey, I clearly see that it has been Christ who has carried me, and it has been Christ who has walked by my side, never forgetting about me, abandoning me, or divorcing me. He has never forsaken me!

When I was a child, my life was so innocent and pure and definitely sheltered from many of life's realities. After my brother's death, my parents became super-protective. However, protected as I was, I was totally unprepared to meet the world and all its painful cruelties and deceptions. My childhood dreams would be shattered as worldly realities came crashing into my life. How could I reckon life when my dreams were falling apart?

My first love was Charlie. I talked about him all the time, and even though we were miles apart, it seemed like everyone who knew me, knew him. Charlie was my world, and he consumed my thoughts and heart. I lived for his calls and dreamed of the times when we could be together. My life was truly a fairy tale come true. I was so much in love, and everyone knew it. But then it was over. *What happened?* I stuffed my grief and emotions and tried not to think about it. I cried so many tears but to no avail—Charlie was gone. He was out of my life. Over and over again, I asked myself, what happened? No explanation, nothing. One moment he was saying I love you, and the next moment, there was silence. I thought my life was over, and I would never be able to love again.

Because life goes on, I dove into my studies. My grades were great, but my social life died. I had no desire to be around people, especially men. It seemed my life had come to an end, so, depressed and alone, I finished my second year of college, just me and my broken heart. I had been so fully alive and vivacious, with such big dreams, but after Charlie walked out of my life, my world seemed to come to an end.

Life had to continue, and three years later I met a wonderful man who met all the qualifications of a good husband and father, and I began dating again. With my self-deceived belief that I couldn't love again, I married Sam, not because I was madly in love with him but because he was a good man. I did love him, but it wasn't the deep kind of love that lasts, and five years and two children later, we were divorced.

All my life I had been good and obedient. I knew, after the loss of my brother and because of mother's "condition," that I needed to make life pleasant for Mom and Dad, not add to their troubles. So I followed all the rules, made good grades, did all the right things, and lived my life in such a way that would gain the favor of both God and man. So why was all this happening to me? Why was everything in my life falling apart? Was God punishing me for something? If so, what? Why had God deserted me? Why wouldn't God step in and help me? First, Charlie left, and now, Sam.

After my divorce in the fall of 1975, with my life in the pit of despair and alone, I once again found myself in the sea of despondency. I was twenty-seven, and my life was over again. I wondered how I could kill myself that wouldn't hurt. I had had enough pain, and I didn't want any more. I just wanted my life to be over.

In the darkness of my den, while my little boys lay napping in their room, I pondered how I would end my life. Speeding into a concrete wall would work, but taking an overdose of Mom's sleeping pills seemed less painful and certainly more effective. It was while I was pondering this, as Barry Manilow's song "You Are My Child" played over and over again on my stereo, that I heard two words: *born again*. I immediately responded, "I'm a Christian! I don't need this born-again fanatic stuff. I have been baptized and confirmed. I sang in the choir and ironed altar cloths." On and on I went, listing all the good things I had done. Again, I heard the words *born again*, and again I presented my arguments. I heard the words a third time, but this time the thought came to me that maybe God wasn't there for me. Maybe, that was the reason my life was falling apart. Maybe I didn't really know what God was all about, and since I didn't want to live anyway, maybe I should give this born-again thing a try. So I said, "If there is anything to this, then just kill me off and move in." Falling on my knees, I asked for help, and for the first time I understood Jesus died for *me*. No one had ever loved me that much! I knew, in that moment, in the depths of my heart, that had I been the only person on the planet, Jesus, my Savior, still would have come and died just for me!

The kids began to stir from their naps, and I needed to prepare dinner, so I attended to their needs, not with a sparkle in my eyes or hope in my heart but with a normal sense of responsibility toward my children. There were no stars, clanging chimes, or trumpets sounding the news that Jesus had saved me, but in heaven, the angels were singing, and Jesus shed tears of joy. Jesus had been trying to reach me for so long, but I hadn't been listening. Within days, God began His confirmation process, and within three years, I saw the birth of a business, a marriage to a man I fell in love with, and a life super-charged with love, hope, and a future; radical changes!

My business took off, and one job led to another, then another. The Holy Spirit was giving me direction and showing me what to do and how to do it. Even math, which has never been my strong suit, seemed to make sense. Formulas and problems seemed easy, even figuring quantities and yardages. God had put me in a field that I had been created to do. It was a design business, in a city where designers were virtually unheard of and where there were no woman-owned interior design businesses. It almost seemed funny to me, yet I knew God had paved a way for me, and with His help, I could do anything. Because I was so poor and only had the help of the Lord, I called upon Him for everything.

More fabric samples were necessary for my new small business. One day I happened to look at the back of a sample book and saw a name, address, and phone number of a fabric supplier. The Lord told me to call, so I did. I scheduled an appointment, and Don Leader, co-owner of a large designer showroom in Minneapolis, showed up about four weeks later. He pulled his Winnebago, which housed his traveling sample showroom, into the Holiday Inn parking lot and called all his established customers, including me. On the day of my appointment, I knocked on the door with a somewhat excited fear. Don, a medium-sized man with dark hair, opened the door. He seemed nonthreatening, so I went in. He began asking me questions right away, finding out who I was and how long I had been in business.

Because God's reality had so infused my life by this time, and because God had miraculously started my business and now had led me to this man, in our initial conversation I mentioned something to Don about the Lord.

Don looked at me with a glint in his eye and asked if I was a "baby Christian." When I said yes, he asked me how long. I said, "Only a few months."

God is so great, and oh, how He loves me. The Lord had personally sent Don to me! He was a wonderful, mature Christian man, who took me under his wing. He asked me if I had a Bible; I didn't. He told me which one to get and where to go to buy it. He let me talk about my pain, listened to my story, and prayed for me. He was sent by God to help me in so many ways. Don became my spiritual mentor, and whenever he was in town, he always took the time to help, teach, and listen to me.

Don told me to bring my little station wagon to Minneapolis, which I did, and gave me a large assortment of samples, all free of charge. Jesus, knew I had no money, and had no idea which companies I would need as vendors, so He intervened and used Don to provide me with the information I needed to get started.

It was in 1976 that I began asking God for a mate. He had given Adam to Eve, so I knew God could and would handpick someone just for me. I had tried on my own to find someone but had failed both times, so this time it had to be God's choice.

One day the phone rang; it was my father. He told me that a friend of his, who owned a motel, had had some fire damage in one of the rooms and asked if I would help redo it. I was to ask for Dick, the man's son. Dick, was not exactly the easiest man to work with, but after he showed me the damaged room, I put together a few possibilities and made my presentation. One was selected, and I proceeded to do the work.

In 1977 my business was growing, and my father told me I needed to have insurance. Obviously, if I was going to be in business, I needed to function responsibly. Dad advised me to see the same friend who owned the motel, who, also had an insurance agency. When I went to fill out the paperwork, Dick, who by now had decided to try the insurance business with his father, was assigned to help me. I still remembered my unfavorable first impression of him, so I told him what I needed and left. He came by my office a few weeks later with the insurance policy, but then, two weeks later he came around again. I assumed, this time, he needed payment, so I wrote him a check. A month later he stopped by again, this time for no reason. I was clueless—I'd received my policy and had paid him, so why was he there?

He told me he wasn't coming by on insurance buisness, but wanted to ask me out for dinner. Startled and totally taken off guard, I accepted but then thought, what have I done? I didn't know this guy and wasn't sure if I wanted to know him. My two sons, Robert and Joe, and I were in such a good place, and because I already had two little boys and a great relationship with the Lord, I didn't know if I needed any one else in my life

Dick and I did go out that night and I saw who he really was—a man behind a mask. He actually was very nice, and I found myself enjoying his company. Over the next few months, I became aware of my increasing affection for Dick; I was falling in love again.

It became clear that God had answered my prayer almost immediately after I prayed, but I had been too blind to see it. God had handpicked Dick just for me. We were in love and got married in the spring of 1978. He had had four children (Mike, Angie, Dede, and Patrick), and I had had the two (Robert and Joseph), so we started our life together with six children. With God on our side, what could come against us? If we had only known …

Looking back, there were many ups and downs in our lives; I could clearly see God working in the midst of them all. You might say that Dick and I grew up together. We raised our children together and had two children of our own (Jonathan and Richard)—eight in all. What a blessing. Has it been easy? Absolutely not. Ninety percent of all second marriages with children end in divorce, but we, by the grace of God, survived.

I had married Dick knowing that he was not born again. I had thought that he couldn't live with me too long without changing; that was my mistake. I was banking on my abilities to persuade and convince Dick. It wasn't about Dick's hard heart; it was about my need to see Dick saved. I had to learn how to reflect Jesus. I had to ask myself, was I reflecting Jesus by giving him Bible verses? Was I reflecting Jesus with my persuasive arguments? Was I reflecting Jesus by pouting or grumbling at Dick when he wouldn't yield to my way of thinking? For nineteen years I prayed for him. For nineteen years I tried to convince him that Jesus was the way. For nineteen years I tried doing it my way, I couldn't get my own husband to surrender to me or to God. What was I doing wrong? Why, Lord? I would fall on my knees and soak the bedspread with my tears on behalf of Dick, Mike, Angie, Dede, and Pat. Robert, Joseph, Jonathan, and Richard had all surrendered their lives to Jesus when the Billy Graham crusade came to town. but nothing had happened to Dick or his four.

In 1995 Dick and I went through a terrible financial crisis. Dick had gone back into the motel business shortly after we married. The motel had become old, along with everything in it. The cost of updating was more than we had, and one thing led to another. With looming debt before us, God sent Dick's close friend, who, purchased the motel and assumed all the debt. The deal allowed Dick to walk away from it all. It was devastating yet a relief for Dick. His entire identity had been built upon the motel, and now it was gone. What could he do? Where could he go? Where were the answers?

He and his sister had talked and agreed that real estate would be an avenue that could provide some future for Dick. I was told of this decision after it was made. I had not been brought into the decisions concerning the motel, and now, once again, I was not brought into the decision concerning his future. How could we have been so close, yet, moved so far apart? "Why Lord?" I cried.

I took on more design projects plus another job, just to help make ends meet. I totally immersed myself into work. I distanced myself from Dick so I would not have to hear about what he was or was not doing. Days would go by, and we would not speak about anything real. When we would talk, the words were sharp, bitter, and harsh. (Failure seems to do that to people.) Life ripped open our hearts and minds and pierced us at the core of who we were. Dick did not want to hear about a loving God; he did not want an optimistic wife. His, was a world where dark voices had more power and influence than anything or anybody.

I pressed closer to God during this time. As previously in my life, when the darkness was all around me, it was only God who picked me up and carried me. I needed to trust Him above all. I had to trust when I didn't see any sign of light at the end of any tunnel, and I had to believe God for the impossible. Fear gripped me! I would sit in my bathtub with the door locked, rocking back and forth, Bible in hand, memorizing Psalm 91 and other verses, just to silence the screams of fear. Since faith comes by hearing, I would speak the Word of God out loud so my ears would hear, and faith would be increased. I spoke and meditated on the Word all the time. I didn't know what else to do.

I begged God to allow me to be involved in Christian work. I didn't know where Dick and I were going, but it looked to me like another divorce was approaching. I desperately wanted to escape and just serve the Lord. In 1996 Pastor Bob Frickholm called me and asked me to begin a prayer ministry in the church. I immediately said yes. My Christian life had always been centered around talking with God, so I knew prayer was where I could best serve. Because I was now to head a prayer ministry, Susan, one of the assistant pastors, thought it wise for me to go to a prayer conference. There was one coming in July that I thought I could attend.

With summer came a paying job opportunity for Dick. He would manage a new hotel being built. Since real estate was never profitable for him, this seemed like the perfect job. It was a venue with which he was most familiar and proficient. The only problem was, the training was the same week as my conference. Regretfully, I had to cancel going so Dick could go to his training. All seemed lost again. I knew I could go on with the prayer ministry, but it would have been so wonderful to get away and get some training. Then Susan called again. There was another prayer and spiritual warfare conference in Saint Louis in September, it was free, and I could go.

September's conference was more than I could have asked for. The first speaker, Ed Silvoso, spoke about why people don't want to come to Jesus. As I listened, God began to open my eyes to a new approach, a biblical evangelistic approach. Why have we, as believers, not seen this? We are to be loving, not judgmental. We are to pray for others, not criticize. We are to ask forgiveness from those we have wronged and not hold grudges. This was the light I needed. I could see it. If I could take this message back to

Sioux Falls and begin to implement this truth, we possibly could see revival in our city. This could actually change lives.

God had opened my eyes to see something much bigger than I ever thought or imagined and after the speaker finished, I wanted to receive prayer from one of the prayer ministers. I found a prayer minister, and as she began to pray, the Lord's voice spoke clearly to me, saying, "Mary, you are harboring anger, bitterness, and unforgiveness against your husband, and I cannot use you until you seek his forgiveness." I said, "But Lord, I've been the one who was silent when he hurled cruel words. I was the one who did not retaliate or stoop to his level." But the Lord came back and said again, "Mary, you are harboring anger, bitterness, and unforgiveness against your husband, and I cannot use you until you seek his forgiveness." The desire to serve the Lord was stronger than the desire to hold on to my anger, bitterness, and unforgiveness toward Dick, so I said, "Yes, Lord." I knew it would be only by God's grace that I could ask forgiveness from Dick. In my eyes, Dick was wrong, but in God's eyes, I was wrong. I was God's child. I knew better.

Dick had responded how this world responds. I had been called to a higher standard and I was to love, forgive, show mercy, and grace. I had anger toward Dick, I was wrong, and I knew it. I had been convicted.

All the way home on the plane, I asked God to help me do what He wanted me to do. All the way home, I prayed for God's strength. The rubber was meeting the road, and I either had to obey or not obey. It was my choice.

Richard and Dick were at the gate when I arrived. I saw Dick. "God, help me." He was toward the back of the crowd with his hands in his pockets and his head slightly raised. I greeted Richard and then walked over to Dick. I put my arms around him and told him I loved him. Walking down the concourse, I held his hand and asked, "When we get home, could we talk?" Once home, he quickly managed to get rid of the kids for a while so we could take a walk alone. On the walk, I confessed that I had been holding anger in my heart toward him for the ugly things he had said to me. I confessed that bitterness had crept into my heart, and that I was guilty of unloving behavior toward him. I hadn't prayed for him because I considered the things he was doing were stupid, and I asked for his forgiveness. I confessed that even though he had been elected to our city council, I had been so angry with him that I hadn't lifted him in prayer as a leader. God had commanded me in his Word to pray for leaders, and I hadn't prayed for him; I had disobeyed God, all out of anger.

Dick became like a marshmallow on a hot day. All powers of evil were defused. God was victorious. His kingdom was activated that day, and His principles of love, forgiveness, grace, and mercy were stamped on our hearts forever. Our marriage was instantly healed. We blessed our home, and, in the presence of our children, spoke new vows to one another. God had done something so miraculous, so amazing, and so divine. Can He put the shattered pieces back together again? Yes. With God, all things are possible. If we live by the sword, we will die by the sword, but if we follow God's ways, then we will live in a kingdom where goodness reigns. He is able to do far more abundantly than we could ever hope or imagine.

With the healing to our marriage came a far deeper love for each other. Instead of lecturing Dick about God, I let God be reflected through me. Instead of evangelizing Dick and pointing out Bible verses, I prayed blessings upon him. I prayed for his felt need. If he was having a meeting at City Hall, I would pray that others would listen to him and understand what he was saying. If Dick was having a rough day, I prayed God would give him grace. If he was suffering with his image, I prayed for God to allow people to see what a true servant he was and how dedicated he was to our city. Each day I would pray with him. God answered those prayers and was slowly revealing Himself to Dick.

Three months after I returned from Saint Louis, I was lying in bed next to Dick, praying blessings over him, while he lay sleeping. God interrupted my prayer with this statement: "Examine the quality of his love for you." As I lay there, meditating on what God had just said to me, the thought came to me that perhaps Dick had asked Jesus into his heart, and I didn't know it. With that thought still fresh in my head, I flicked on the light and rolled him over onto his back. I asked him, "Did you ask Jesus into your heart, and you didn't tell me?" He started to open his eyes and ask me what I was saying. Again, I said, "Did you ask Jesus into your heart, and you didn't tell me?" As he was trying to get to a level of consciousness, I asked again.

This time he responded, "I don't know."

"Well, if you don't know, do you want to know?"

"Okay," he answered.

I couldn't believe it. I had prayed for this moment for nineteen years, and now he willingly said okay. I don't know what prayer we prayed or how we said it, but I do know that God worked a miracle in our lives.

If God's ways are lived out, the world will see. There is life after death, but it is not through anything we say or do. Life is birthed because people see God and are touched by His love, mercy, goodness, and grace.

Chapter 2

WORD, VISION, VICTORY

In the fall of 2003, as I was in prayer, God spoke and said, *"Mary, I am going to take you places you do not want to go and have you go through things you do not want to go through."* Being alarmed by this message, I went to Pastor Susan to see what this might mean. Unfortunately, I learned nothing, so I waited.

One morning, weeks later, I received an open vision. I saw myself very clearly in the middle of the ocean. I was looking around, wondering how on earth I had gotten there. Since I have always been frightened of the ocean, I was surprised that I did not feel terrorized. Then I woke up. When I asked the Lord about the meaning of the vision, he told me, *"The kingdom of God is like floating in the ocean."*

I said, "I don't know what that means."

"Can you stand?" He asked.

"No, Lord, the ocean floor is miles down, and even if I tried to stand, I would sink."

"That's right." Then He asked me, *"Can you swim?"*

I answered, "Yes, but Lord, which way would I go? I could be swimming away from land instead of swimming toward it."

"That's right." Then He said, *"The kingdom of God is like floating in the ocean. You are going to have to trust Me."*

With that, I felt an overwhelming sense that His hands would be under me, keeping me from sinking, and His Spirit would blow me where He wanted me to go.

And It Began

Psalm 91 has long been one of my favorites; being sheltered by Him is exactly where I want to be. With my life falling apart and without any ability to stop what was happening, my only refuge was the time I spent with God. From the bringing of my season of trials, in January 2004, until now, as I write this, God alone has been my help. There were too many occurrences to list them all, but I'll share a few that were amongst the most heartbreaking.

I'm a dog lover, and over a period of five years, I lost all three of my precious springer spaniels: one to old age, one through loneliness during our separation in Minneapolis, and one three-year-old to cancer. In 2005, I closed my five-thousand square foot retail store, and moved to a smaller location that offered interior design services only. Stress over closing and relocating my business, was overwhelming! Every arthritic joint within my body became inflamed, which made moving and renovating the new space extremely difficult and painful; emotionally and physically. In my twenties, I had been diagnosed with osteoarthritis and had been constantly dealing with joint issues. After exhausting all known treatments, I finally had to have the necessary surgeries—two knee replacements, a hip replacement, and an extensive lower back surgery. With each surgery, there were complications and more pain—before, during, and post-op.

The city ministry I was leading, which brought interdenominational intercessors together, split apart. Without understand why God had allowed this, I rested on my presumptions which caused a deep wound in my heart. Our home, which sits on top of a hill, was hit by two different storms, which flooded our basement both times. Not only was it expensive to clean and replace but it was also extremely difficult on my bones. While dealing with the many thing tumbling down around me, my father, who had been diagnosed with Alzheimer's, became a constant challenge. He was sun-downing plus having other behavioral issues which made finding a safe memory care facility difficult. We moved him in and out of many different facilities and no matter where he was, Mom and I would travel for regular visits. One cold day in February he fell and broke his hip. Two weeks later my wonderful dad, who had meant the world to me, died without knowing my name.

Mom and Dad had been married for over fifty years, and both had become dependent on my brother and me. After Dad died, mom became a full-time job. She developed another cancerous tumor and never was able to deal with the grief and loneliness, and three years later, she died. The following year, doctors diagnosed me with a rare fatal disease, which explained other symptoms I had been experiencing, and I had to begin treatments.

My husband, Dick caught a virus in October of 2004 which attacked his heart, giving him congestive heart failure, and after six months of diminished energy, he was given a pacemaker. Five years later, we had to temporarily move to Minneapolis for him to prepare and receive a left ventricle heart pump (LVAD). We knew the LVAD would only be a temporary fix, but it allowed us to move back to Sioux Falls. While on the LVAD, he had a stroke, which took us back to Minneapolis. Ten months later, as both his ventricles were failing, we received the call; they had a heart. So, in July 2011, Dick had a heart transplant.

In the summer of 2014, my younger brother was having difficulty breathing and after tests, was diagnosed with stage-four lung cancer. My sister Beverly, moved to Sioux Falls and together we cared for our dear brother. He had no wife or children, so my home became his hospice for the last three months of his life. He died in his old bedroom in our family home.

With so many serious challenges in my life, actually one on top of the other, many of my casual friends had moved on with their lives, which saddened me, and my close friends were growing weary. I wasn't able to work as much as I had been, and with Dick unable to work during his heart failure years, our finances took a real hit. During the time when my brother was dying, my right foot had become crippled. So in January 2016, I had to have a total foot reconstruction—detaching the Achilles tendon, repairing the heel, repairing and reattaching the Achilles tendon, and cutting muscles in my calf. It was a major surgery, one from which I am still recovering as of this writing.

God *alone* has been carrying me. His Word to me was true! There was no way I could stand on my own, and I had no way of knowing where I was going. *I had to learn to float!* Had God not told me ahead of time that I would be going through these trials, I would have thought I was cursed, like Job.

I've heard it called the *dark days of the soul*, and that is an accurate description. The perfect storm that hit my life, relentlessly kept pounding me emotionally and physically, but spiritually, it was making me stronger. Is God enough? Yes. I disciplined myself to spend hours with the Lord, thinking about who He was and staying in His Word. I purposely focused my mind and attention on others and prayer. It was not easy. I had many moments of deep anguish with gut-wrenching inner torment with my tears soaking the floor. I sounded more like Jeremiah lamenting than David, singing sweet songs of praise. "How, oh Lord, do I get through this?" I anguished. "Help me."

Step by step, I inched forward until trusting became a part of my nature. As I endured trial after trial, although, all were devastating, each successive one became a little less painful. I dwelled in that secret place and ate the Word. God actually became the shelter covering me and the ground beneath my feet, and it was only His Spirit who provided the cool breezes for my relief. Questions of why He would allow these trials, disappeared from my mind as I remembered the vision and how I was to survive. He had said, "Trust Me!"

In January 2004, God's words spoken to me began. Living through these years seemed like a horrible, heart-wrenching nightmare. But now, as I look back on those day, I finally am able to see those trials as blessings. Blessings, that have opened my eyes and given me the ability to identify with others in their grief, and, blessings, which have taken me far deeper with the Lord than I could have ever imagined.

I'm hopeful, that the meditations and journal entries that helped me on my journey, can also help others. Be blessed.

Chapter 3

WORTH

What is your worth? Meditate upon your life.
Is it precious or can it be discarded? Now, ask the Lord
to show you how He sees you and meditate upon it.
"We are God's masterpiece" Selah
Ephesians 2:10 (NLT)

Bear with each other and forgive whatever grievances you may have
against one another. Forgive as the Lord forgave you and over all these
virtues put on love, which binds them all together in perfect unity.
—Colossians 3:13–14 (NIV)

What does it mean to ascribe worth? To me, it is to intentionally establish
value on a person or thing. What God considers valuable may be something
entirely different from what we consider valuable. This value system
determines what we do and how we act. What is valuable—our neighbors,
families, jobs, homes, or cars? Is ascribing worth to someone or something
an act of love? What takes precedence in our day? Is love the motivator
behind our efforts throughout the day?

Imagine needing a new pair of glasses and the time and energy it takes
to find the right pair. We may try on many different frames before finally
selecting one. We ascribe importance to our eyesight and appearance, so we
undertake the task. The same holds true when looking for a place to live.
Our homes, where we stay during our time away from work, is important
to us, so we hunt for the right place and spend our hard-earned money on
a place to live, then also invest out time and energy to make it our own.

Eyeglasses and homes are things that are important but will ultimately
be destroyed. What about people—a spouse, a child, a friend, or a neighbor?
What is their value? Our eyesight and homes are important, but Jesus did
not put Calvary's worth on things but on people.

How much is a neighbor worth? Is he or she worth your time and
energy? The entire planet is full of hurting people who need to know the
love of God, not through our talk but through our walk. At the cross,
Calvary's love brought into focus the immensity of lavished love, walked
out, proclaiming God's great worth for us. It transcends all ordinary means
of measurement.

Love must be the core essential that infuses and stimulates prayer. We
are urged to love more fervently because love covers a multitude of sins.
Love's covering hides faults and bears burdens; it forgives and forgets. If
I love someone, I will pray for that person. I will give attention to those

things that I see as valuable. If prayers are not rooted in love, they are just a religious exercise. Is love the propelling force behind what we do?

A friend once said, "If we loved everyone around us all the time and were attentive to their needs, we wouldn't get anything done." That may be true, but that's what Christ did. He is calling each of us, not necessarily to do but to love. It may come as a smile, an encouraging word, a compliment, a demonstration of grace, a helping hand, forgiveness, an act of love, or a prayer, but each day put on love. Wear God's glasses, which allows you to see the true worth of a soul. Everywhere you go and with everyone you speak, ascribe worth, and let God's love, which is inside you, flow out to them all.

Finest Masterpiece

For we are God's handiwork, created in Christ Jesus to do good works,
which God prepared in advance for us to do.
—Ephesians 2:10 (NLT)

A study conducted on mice at the University of California in Los Angeles reported researchers' discovery of tiny nerves crisscrossing the spine that can be used to bypass crippling injuries. It is nothing short of a revelation to imagine the central nervous system rewiring itself. These tiny nerves act much like a detour on a highway. God created us in such a way that even tiny nerves stand by to repair if injured. Spinal cord injuries, written off as irreversible, may someday be repaired. Everything down to the smallest cell has a purpose. Skin cells are positioned in the correct place and do the job they were designed to do. The same is true with finger cells, stomach cells, thyroid cells, and so on; every part in the body has the intended cell for its appropriate area, and there are even back-up nerves and extra ligaments that can be used, if needed. Human beings are no accident. Imagine God creating His finest masterpiece without a purpose—it makes no sense. Inventors create machines for a reason, not just to sit on a shelf.

The Bible talks about purpose, good works, and destiny, and Paul, in his letter to the Ephesians, actually says God planned ahead of time for us to do good work. That suggests we were in God's mind long before we were born, and He has something He wants each of us to do. God thought about you and wanted you to do something. *Selah.* That should make you feel special, you are part of His amazing plan! *Selah.*

Christ paved the way for us to reach our destiny and discover our jobs. He has made some apostles, prophets, evangelists, pastors, and teachers. He has made some to be in business, some to be in the home, some to be caregivers or protectors, some to be inside a church, some inside the arts, some in the city, and some on the farm. There are billions of people, all with a good work destined by God. Every human is unique and will have a unique combination of DNA, gifts, and talents. Amazing—if you think about it, there are no duplicates. How can you use your uniqueness to bring glory to God? How can you stay unique to do the good work that only you can do?

When was the last time you sat down and gave thanks for all God has given you, the seen and unseen? And when was the last time you thought of how everything in life has meaning and purpose. There is a destiny designed specifically for each of us. What do you enjoy, and what is in your heart for you to become? How has God already prepared you to do these things?

Now, with God's help, step out in faith into your destiny.

Freedom

> Therefore if any man *be* in Christ,
> *he is* a new creature: old things are passed away;
> behold, all things are become new.
> — 2 Corinthians 5:17 (KJV)

How wonderful to be absolutely free to be whoever we were meant to be; to be able to look at others not through the conditional lenses of our minds but to see as Christ sees.

Personal worth or identity typically reflects what we or others think; it's a man-made value system based upon the events, family, and personal history that has shaped our lives. If these warped beliefs were to be removed, we might be able to see ourselves as God sees us. In truth, however, very few of us actually see ourselves as beautiful creations. It's easier, in this world, to see the flaws and ugliness of life. So how can we get God's perspective?

When something defines what can or cannot be done, then that thing is calling the shots. Our worth should come from God and not from institutional expectations or human ideals. If a believer can be manipulated by others' expectations, or if cruel words bring despair and discouragement, then that believer is not free. He or she believes the lie.

The Lord wills for all to be saved that none be lost; the old is to fade, and the new is to emerge. The Lord will always love, encourage, and accept you just as you are. He shows no preference for male or female, rich or poor, Jew or Gentile. His heart is always to protect and provide. The world may have seen fit to beat you up, but the *you inside* is the masterpiece God created. He does not make mistakes. Let the Holy Spirit help the *you inside* find your way to the truth. Ask yourself, "Is it possible to believe what God says about me, in spite of the criticism and self-imposed negativity swirling around in my brain? Is it possible for me to break away from the belief I have developed over a lifetime? Is it possible to allow the Holy Spirit to be mightier than my human instincts and habits?"

God says, "All things are possible."

> Husbands, love your wives, just as Christ loved the church
> and gave himself up for her to make her holy, *cleansing*
> her by the washing with water through the word, and to
> present her to himself as a radiant church, without stain or
> wrinkle or any other blemish, but holy and blameless.
> —Ephesians 5:25–27 (NIV, emphasis added)

> However, as it is written: "No eye has seen, no ear has heard, no mind
> has conceived what God has prepared for those who love him."
> —1 Corinthians 2:9 (NIV)

In the Ephesians passage, Paul twice uses the word *holy*. It is the same word but with two very different meanings. Paul uses a husband/wife relationship to make a spiritual comparison. Husbands are to love their wives *as Christ loves us* and gave Himself up for us, His church, making her holy. *The word* holy *refers to an object that is only sanctified when God Himself designates it as belonging to Him.*

A man falls head over heels in love and courts and marries his love. She is the only one he sees, and just as she is the only one for him, he too is the only one for her. Mutual love binds the two in their exclusive relationship.

If a woman is truly loved, there is nothing she will not do for the one she loves. Likewise, if a man is truly loved, there is no limit to the level of protection and care he will provide. A godly marriage is a beautiful picture of Christ and His bride. The husband, Christ, has washed His bride and presented her to Him as a radiant, innocent, virginal bride, without stain or wrinkle, *holy* and blameless.

This second use of the word *holy* means *that which has been brought into relationship with God and designated by Him as having a sacred purpose or special significance to Him.* Your unconditional sacrificial lover has set you apart to be His own. You are His, and He is yours. He has washed away your past because of His unfathomable love for you. There is a sacred purpose for your life that He designated only you would fulfill.

The level of your love for God is proportional to the understanding of His love for you.

More than a Carpenter

"Where did this man get these things?" they asked. "What's this wisdom that has been given him, that he even does miracles! Isn't this the carpenter? Isn't this Mary's son and the brother of James, Joseph, Judas and Simon? Aren't his sisters here with us?"
And they took offense at him."
—Mark 6:3 (NIV)

It is not easy to work with people who have known you from your childhood; it is very difficult for them to see you as an adult. Neighbors of Jesus couldn't see past His young, familiar face. Why would anyone think He had something life-changing to say?

Our human nature tells us we learn from adults, not vice versa. A child is not supposed to have adult wisdom and understanding, unless, of course, that child happens to have lived in the heavens before the creation of the world and just so happens to be the Creator Himself. But how would anyone have known or even suspected Jesus was the incarnate God? Jesus's neighbors couldn't see that He was the King of all kings. To them, he was just another carpenter's apprentice, someone they passed on the street or met at work. What could he possibly show them? They didn't know he was the Messiah; no one suspected it. To them, he was simply a carpenter—Mary's boy.

Was anyone watching for the Messiah? If so, what were they expecting? History tells us that they were waiting for a leader who would conquer the Romans and lift the Roman oppression from the Jews—a kingly messiah who would right all wrongs. Jesus, by all observances, was an ordinary-looking man who had no resemblance to that of a king. Could someone who appears to be common be anything but common? *Selah.*

It is hard for me to imagine how Jesus's friends and neighbors could not see how different He was. He always had to be good, certainly not a normal kid, a frustration to His siblings due to His always being perfect, always kind, always right. *Selah.*

There are people all around us who God created. Do we see them? Look at them. What are their talents? Examine their value. Don't let assumption fool you. They may be more than they appear to be.

Undeserving

I often find that God speaks to me through the ordinary experiences in my life. My oldest son is a wonderful young man who works so hard and gives his best in everything he does. Everyone loves Robert, and there isn't anything he wouldn't do for anyone. He shows genuine love, goodness, kindness, and mercy to people all the time. That is who he is.

He had cared about a certain young lady years earlier, and during the Thanksgiving holiday she had showed signs of a renewed affection toward him. He had wooed her with flowers, candlelight dinners, and notes when they first went together, and now with a renewed chance and great expectations, joy was rising in my son.

As Christmas drew near, the romance that had started years earlier was rekindled. Robert was coming home for Christmas, first landing in Minneapolis to see her before coming home to South Dakota. Last night I phoned his brother Richard, who lives in Minneapolis, to inquire when they were coming home and discovered that the young lady had not seen Robert. He had tried to call her several times but without success. It was obvious, she was avoiding him.

After listening to Richard, I said, "*She doesn't deserve my son!*" When I heard myself say that, I realized I could relate with God. How the Father longs for humankind to know His Son, Jesus! I knew what a wonderful husband my son Robert would have been to this young woman, and God fully knows the extravagant love His Son wants to give to His bride. *Selah.*

What a wonderful Son God has and how genuinely He cares. If only the bride could see Him as the Father does. If only she would stop avoiding Him, love Him, and experience His love. If only she would answer the phone or open the door. The groom stands knocking. She is avoiding Him. And at what point does the Father say, "*She doesn't deserve my Son*"?

There is a world that doesn't know Jesus. It is blind to how wonderful He is. God gave Him to us, not because we deserve Him but because He loves us.

For those who are perishing, time is short. It is my prayer that people will stop avoiding this wonderful Savior and experience the love He wants to give them. It is my prayer they will answer the door and welcome Him in.

Who Is My Neighbor?

And behold, a certain lawyer stood up, and tempted him saying,
Master, what shall I do to inherit eternal life? He said unto
him, What is written in the law? How does it read to you?
And he answered and said, You shall love the Lord your God with
all your heart, and with all your soul, and with all, your strength,
and with all your mind; and your neighbor as yourself. And He said
to him, You have answered correctly; Do this and you will live. But
wishing to justify himself, he said to Jesus, and who is my neighbor?
—Luke 10:25–27 (KJV)

But I say to you who hear: Love your enemies, do
good to those who hate you, bless those who curse
you, and pray for those who mistreat you.
—Luke 6:27–28 (NASB)

The young man, trying to justify himself, asked, "Who is my neighbor?" In other words, who must I love? We all can love people whose views are similar to ours or who are sweet, kind, and pleasant to be around, but how about those who are on the other side of the political or social fence? Could they, along with drunks and terrorists, be classified as our neighbors? Should any of these be expendable and excluded from love? At any time did Jesus ever let us off the hook regarding whom we were to love? If we are honest with ourselves, every day we allocate worth to each person with whom we come into contact. Do away with selective loving, and look upon every person through the eyes of God.

The question shouldn't be *who do I need to love*" but *who do I get to love?* We are to love our neighbors, our enemies, and those who despitefully use us. There is not a reason *not* to love. Take your thoughts captive, agree with God, and lovingly reach out to all those who surround you. The Word says, God so loved the world that He gave His Son—that is an unimaginable love! It is not up to us to defensively argue or justify love. It is up to us to submit to God's will and live it. Today, walk obediently in loving kindness. Evil cannot stand against it, and love will get the victory.

Chapter 4

HEART

What do you treasure? What is it that you desire most?

"where your treasure is, there your heart will be also."
Selah
Matthew 6:21 (NIV)

Assumption

The Old Testament speaks of people who were unfaithful to God. They assumed the grain would come and the harvest would produce fruit, and they could live their lives as they wanted without consequence. Assumption is a deception. Too often it is based on a lie from the enemy. The truth is there are consequences when we do not listen to God and are not submitted to His ways.

God, through the prophet Hosea, says, "She has not acknowledged that I was the one who gave her the grain, the new wine and oil, who lavished on her the silver and gold which they used for Baal. Therefore I will take away my grain when it ripens, and my new wine when it is ready. I will take back my wool and my linen, intended to cover her naked body" (Hosea 2:8–9 NIV).

God saw the religious unbelief of Israel, and His response to their displaced worship was to remove His hand and let them provide for themselves. Lest we see our human efforts as futility and acknowledge that God protects, defends, and supplies all of our needs, we too may be left to fend for ourselves.

I believe that believers have come through a time where their faith has been tested—a season where battles have been fought, and many in the body are beaten, bruised, and weakened. Many have come to a place where their eyes have been opened to their own selfish ambitions and personal efforts. God is not interested in personal ambitions and efforts. He is building a kingdom, and He desires us to love Him with all our hearts, souls, minds, and strengths. As humans, we must be in need of mercy before we appreciate mercy, must be in need of grace before appreciating grace, and must become desperate for God before we seek His reality and faithfulness. Trusting God when our eyes cannot see is difficult, but we need to acquire the ability in the days to come. Believing and trusting God to be God and holding Him to His Word is an act of faith, and we are called to be people of faith, not sight.

Just as in the days of Hosea, restoration is available. "I will show my love to the one I called 'Not my loved one.' I will say to those called Not my people,' You are my people' and they will say, 'You are my God" (Hosea 2:23 NIV). We *are* His people, and we can trust Him.

Do not let personal efforts, assumptions, or religion steal a true relationship with the King of all kings. Experiencing His supernatural provision, protection, grace, mercy, and love is priceless. Trust in God, and He will direct your path. Do not worry or be anxious for anything, but pray and let the peace of God, which surpasses all understanding, guard your heart and your mind in Christ.

My prayer is that Christ will dwell in your heart by faith and that you will be deeply rooted and established in love. I pray you truly can comprehend the breadth, length, height, and depth of His love for you and be filled with all the fullness of God.

Attitude of the Heart

> David replied, "Against you, you only, have I sinned
> and done what is evil in your sight."
> —Psalm 51:4 (NIV)

> Saul replied, "I have sinned. But please honor me before
> the elders of my people and before Israel; come back with
> me, so that I may worship the LORD your God."
> —1 Samuel 15:30 (NIV)

Make a tree good and its fruit will be good, or make a tree bad and its fruit will be bad, for a tree is recognized by its fruit. You brood of vipers, how can you who are evil say anything good? For out of the overflow of the heart the mouth speaks. The good man brings good things out of the good stored up in him, and the evil man brings evil things out of the evil stored up in him. But I tell you that men will have to give account on the day of judgment

for every careless word they have spoken. For by your words you will be acquitted, and by your words you will be condemned.
—Matthew 12:33–37 (NIV)

Broken people typically do not concern themselves with appearances; rather, they demonstrate true remorse. Grief over their sin weighs so heavily upon them that their freedom can only come when forgiveness and reconciliation are granted. The heart reveals the essence of a person and out of that heart flow words. If King Saul's heart had been pure, his actions would have indicated such. He was playing games with God, as if God would overlook it, but rebellion is rebellion, and Saul's heart was revealed by his words and his disobedience. King David, on the other hand, truly was remorseful when caught in sin.

Saul and David were two men with two entirely different types of hearts. One king grieved over his sin, while the other king wanted to save face. King David cared what God thought, while King Saul cared what people thought. One looked up, while the other looked inward. One was focused on the Lord, while the other was focused on himself. It was fear of God versus fear of man.

When my sons were growing up, they made mistakes, but when caught, sincere tears, sad expressions, and confessions spoke volumes. When they were rebellious, that too was obvious. There was no question the kids were sinners, yet their attitudes revealed their hearts. It might be easy to hide sin, but why would we? *Selah.* Shouldn't we want to walk uprightly? Do we want to surrender to God's will or our will? Do we want to obey or rebel?

David was a man after God's own heart, a man who wrote love songs while tending sheep, who knew God, and who had the courageous confidence to go before Goliath, yet who could pray, "Create in me a clean heart, O God, And renew a right spirit within me. Do not cast me away from your presence and do not take your Holy Spirit from me" (Psalm 51:10 KJV). David, strong yet tender, knew and honored God above all, and God moved on his behalf.

Love the Lord with your whole heart, and get to know Him. He is there for you, and no matter what giant comes toward you, the Lord will move on your behalf.

Just as it was in the days of Noah, so also will it be in the days
of the Son of Man. People were eating, drinking, marrying
and being given in marriage up to the day Noah entered
the ark. Then the flood came and destroyed them all.
—Luke 17:26–27 (NIV)

But the LORD said to Samuel, "Do not look at his appearance
or at the height of his stature, because I have rejected him;
for God sees not as man sees, for man looks at the outward
appearance, but the LORD looks at the heart."
—1 Samuel 16:7 (NASB)

In the days of Noah, wickedness was great, and evil was everywhere. The people corrupted God's worship and filled the earth with violence. They were self-indulgent and infused with every form of wicked behavior.

Anyone could see that the wickedness in humans was great, but God saw that every imagination, or purpose, of the human heart was evil. Humans' hearts were deceitful and desperately wicked, and there was no good among them. Their hearts were deceived and callous; it was a heart condition. God does not see as we see. Humans look upon the flesh and are easily deceived, but God goes much deeper and sees the real truth, looking into our hearts.

Are we living in a society similar to the days of Noah? Is our world, with all its glitz and glamour, filled with wickedness, violence, and evil? Let us not be caught ignoring the warnings. Guard your heart from the marketing tools of this world—those tantalizing snares of the fowler that bring only destruction. Pray the Lord will open your eyes to the deception within your heart, and let the peace of God, which passes all understanding, guard your heart and your mind in Christ Jesus.

Beautiful in the Eyes of God

How beautiful on the mountains are the feet of those who bring
good news, who proclaim peace, who bring good tidings, who
proclaim salvation, who say to Zion, "Your God reigns!"
—Isaiah 52:7 (NIV)

How beautiful you are, you who pray and who bring good news to those
whose hearts are open. How beautiful are the feet of those who wear the
shoes of peace. How beautiful are those who pray life to those who are
dead, speak hope to those who are hopeless, pray health to those who are
deceased, and share goodness to those who are in despair. May our God
who reigns, reign with power and wisdom in your life.

And how can they preach unless they are sent? As it is written, "How
beautiful are the feet of those who bring good news!" (Romans 10:15 NIV).

Personal Relationship

Bless those who persecute you; bless and do not curse. Rejoice
with those who rejoice; mourn with those who mourn. Live in
harmony with one another. Do not be proud, but be willing to
associate with people of low position. Do not be conceited. Do
not repay anyone evil for evil. Be careful to do what is right in the
eyes of everyone. If it is possible, as far as it depends on you,
live at peace with everyone.
—Romans 12:14–18 (NIV)

Love is patient and kind. It doesn't envy or boast and is not
proud. Neither does it dishonor others nor is self-seeking, it is

not easily angered or remembers wrongs. Love delights in truth
not in evil. It always protects, trusts, hopes, and perseveres.
—1 Corinthians 13:4–7 (paraphrased)

There are many in today's world who no longer view Christianity in a positive manner, and it seems that the days of a general acceptance of Jesus Christ are fading. The Bible is questioned and non-Christians are vehement in their own views and will passionately argue their beliefs. Whether atheist, Muslim, Buddhist, agnostic, Unitarians, or any other religion or denomination, they all will say their belief is correct. In today's world, independent relativistic opinions are expressed boldly. Anyone with passionate religious views is considered either an extremist or a fanatic, and people no longer want to be subjected to those people. How, then, will Christians lead others to Christ if people will not listen? *Selah.*

It has been my longstanding opinion that if a relationship is motivated by evangelism, there will be little lasting fruit. Relationships must be motivated by love. Love cannot be manufactured; it must be real. If you truly understand the love Christ has for you, your heart will overflow naturally, and it is this genuine overflow of love for a neighbor, friend, or relative that will touch their hearts. Loving takes time and sacrifice.

In our attempts to see people saved, we want instantaneous results, bypassing Jesus's teaching in Luke 10 to first bless, then build relationships, then pray, and last but not least, tell them the good news. Are we so busy that we don't have time for people anymore? *Selah.* Has the relationship process been replaced with texts and e-mails? To have a friend, you must be a friend, and friendship takes time. Trust and respect between two people, over time, will open doors to a lasting relationship that always leads to deep conversations. It will take patience, prayer, and commitment on your part, but how else is the world going to know about Christ? Let your life replace words and your actions tell His story of love.

From one man he made every nation of men, that they should inhabit the whole earth; and he determined the times set for them and the exact places where they should live.
—Acts 17:26 (NIV)

The good man brings good things out of the good stored up in him, and the evil man brings evil things out of the evil stored up in him. But I tell you that men will have to give account on the day of judgment for every careless word they have spoken.
—Matthew 12:35–37 (NIV)

I read once that there are three things that never come back—time, words, and opportunity. We have been designated to be alive at this exact moment in time, in this particular city, in this particular state.

The life of a minute is sixty seconds. Think of how quickly each second ticks away, without much thought. Worldly opportunities come and go, but kingdom opportunities are always working together simultaneously. What we do with each moment is our choice. Our days are filled with actions and reactions, and the complexities of how it all works is incomprehensible. We don't need to understand how it works, but we do need to understand that what we say and do matters. Our words and actions are not insignificant.

It is a privilege to show mercy and grace. Every day we have opportunities to extend a helping hand, a listening ear, or an encouraging word. Since God is sovereign and desires that none shall perish, He always is designing ways for you to be part of His plan in someone's life. We can deliberately bring Christ like responses into every moment. I work in the marketplace, and my days are filled with opportunities to impact my world and to excel at what I do. I always pray for the people I'm going to be seeing, asking God to show me what they would like. It's amazing to see the combinations come together. Prayer and giving your best is an act of worship and when you follow godly ways in business, people know they can trust you. How comforting it is to be able to trust someone. Be Christ like, yet be normal. Remember that people who hire you want a good job, not a sermon. Believe me, they will notice you are different, and, God willing, they will establish a relationship with you.

Jesus influenced each moment of every day through the power of the Holy Spirit. He has given to each of us this same Holy Spirit and has told us that this Spirit will help us do what He did. His words and actions came out of His heart, and no one in history has impacted this world more than Jesus Christ. The psalmist wrote, "Cleanse my heart Oh God and renew a right Spirit within me."

Becoming aware of time, words, and opportunities is vital for the advancement of the kingdom of God. This day matters; your actions matter. Wake up every morning with the awareness of the fresh opportunities that await you. Be expectant, and make the most of this day and every day.

Two Men

One of the criminals who hung there hurled insults at him: 'Aren't you the Christ? Save yourself and us!' But the other criminal rebuked him. 'Don't you fear God,' he said, 'since you are under the same sentence? We are punished justly, for we are getting what our deeds deserve. But this man has done nothing wrong.' Then he said, 'Jesus, remember me when you come into your kingdom. Jesus answered him,' I tell you the truth, today you will be with me in paradise.'
—Luke 23:39–43 (NIV)

Since we have now been justified by his blood, how much
more shall we be saved from God's wrath through him! For if,
when we were God's enemies, we were reconciled to him
through the death of his Son, how much more, having been reconciled,
shall we be saved through his life! Not only is this so, but
we also rejoice in God through our Lord Jesus Christ,
through whom we have now received reconciliation.
—Romans 5:9–11 (NIV)

Two men were hanging beside Jesus, both guilty and condemned to die. One was saved; the other wasn't. One looked hopefully to Christ and asked to be remembered, while the other mocked Him. Scripture says Jesus died for all humankind and has reconciled the whole world to the Father (Colossians 1:20) and predestined us to be adopted through Jesus (Ephesians 1:5). These verses clearly state that God has reconciled and predestined humankind to Himself. God the Father has opened the door and has allowed all who believe access. However, to believe and become a child of God is a choice we each will make. Because we have free will, the decision to believe or not to believe is ours. *Selah* Why do some yield and others don't? Are some more apt to submit than others? *Selah.* We have gained access, but the question is, will we, in faith believe?

I believe the one thief gives us a clue why some yield and others don't. The one thief, speaking to the other, said, "Don't you fear God?" Scripture says the beginning of wisdom is to fear God. I suspect this man grew up in a Jewish home, listening to the teaching about almighty God. Because Jews were awaiting their Messiah, he would have been familiar with the characteristic of the coming Savior. Could it be, that the fear of God comes when we ponder God and compare our own inability, inadequacy, and failure with God's all-sufficient holiness? *Selah.* When goodness is looking at us, we see our own lack. Could it be that this thief looked upon Jesus hanging next to him and, perhaps for the first time, received an understanding that salvation was bigger than earthly battles with earthly foes? This Jesus hadn't been in prison with the other criminals. There were no angry, hateful, vindictive words spewing from His mouth, and He embodied everything that was good. He had done nothing to deserve death. Could he have understood for the first time that he was gazing into the eyes of God?

The other thief appeared to be thinking only about himself as he spewed harsh words.

At the cross that day, both men were reconciled to God, but one neither relinquished his bitterness nor humbled himself, while the other understood he deserved death and asked to be remembered. Two men: one thief saw himself; the other thief saw God. Two men: both reconciled but only one saved.

Chapter 5

PEACE

*Can you be still? Selah   Quiet your soul and
let Christ quiet the storm. Selah*

"Peace, be still!" Selah
Mark 4:39 (ESV)

A Better Portion

As Jesus and his disciples were on their way, he came to a village
where a woman named Martha opened her home to him. She had
a sister called Mary, who sat at the Lord's feet listening to what he
said. But Martha was distracted by all the preparations that had to
be made. She came to him and asked, "Lord, don't you care that
my sister has left me to do the work by myself? Tell her to help
me!" "Martha, Martha," the Lord answered, "you are worried and
upset about many things, but only one thing is needed. Mary has
chosen what is better, and it will not be taken away from her."
—Luke 10:38–42 (NIV)

In a Martha world, busyness, obligations, and commitments overwhelm us
and leave little time to rest. If we truthfully examined our lives, we would
find that commitments and responsibilities demand most of our time. It's
as if our freedom has been lost.

Most Christians have several full-time jobs, including occupation, spouse,
children, parents, church work, ministry commitments, social obligations,
and personal physical care. There are only so many hours in a day, so is it
any wonder that stress-related illnesses and conditions—like heart disease,
anxiety, depression, arthritis, alcoholism, high blood pressure, autoimmune
diseases, and panic attacks—are on the rise? Our busy schedules are hurting
us, and the stress is causing us to miss precious time with Jesus. Our jobs,
family, and ministry are to be a blessing, not a curse.

Jesus came to Mary and Martha's home, and Martha missed it because
she was busy with so many things. Mary, on the other hand, rejected her
traditional expected responsibilities and joined the men on the floor at
Jesus's feet. She said no to the expectations and refused to miss her time
with Him. Jesus said, "Mary has chosen what is better, and it will not be
taken away from her." I wonder what would have happened if both Mary
and Martha had neglected the food preparation. *Selah.* Would the others
have judged them for not doing their "job"? Was Jesus only there for lunch?
I'm sure Jesus could have cared less about a meal. He cared more for those
who were hungry for Him.

"Therefore I tell you, do not worry about your life, what you will eat;

or about your body, what you will wear. For life is more than food, and the body more than clothes. Consider the ravens: They do not sow or reap, they have no storeroom or barn; yet God feeds them. And how much more valuable you are than birds! Who of you by worrying can add a single hour to your life. Since you cannot do this very little thing, why do you worry about the rest?" (Luke 12:22–26 NIV).

So how do we juggle everything? There are meals to make and responsibilities to meet, *but* don't neglect your quiet time with the Lord. Quiet time is what is needed to get you through the day. What in your schedule could be eliminated? Find time to sit at His feet and just *be*; you need it. It is food for your soul, and sitting quietly with Jesus, resting in His presence, does more than you know. Examine your life, and don't be troubled with many things, as only one thing is needed. Choose the better thing.

Peace

Peace I leave with you; my peace I give you. I do not give to you as the world gives. Do not let your hearts be troubled and do not be afraid.
—John 14:27 (NIV)

One of our jobs is to bring peace into the storms of life. It is not our job to labor with the doubt, fear, and chaos that pesters us. Loosen the peace of God from within, and transform the atmosphere around you.

The apostle Paul writes, "I know what it is to be in need, and I know what it is to have plenty. I have learned the secret of being content in any and every situation, whether well fed or hungry, whether living in plenty or in want ... And my God will supply all your needs according to His riches in glory in Christ Jesus" (Philippians 4:19 NASB).

Bring peace into your environment today, and trust God to supply all your needs, according to His riches in glory. "Be still my heart and know that I am God." Jesus came to bring peace—not the peace of this world but the peace that surpasses all comprehension; a peace that will guard your heart and mind in Christ Jesus.

Once I saw a mother, filled with anger, scolding her little child as the child struggled to keep up as they walked toward the entrance to our fairgrounds. My heart was filled with compassion for the child, and I began to pray for peace to come upon that mother. Almost instantaneously, I saw that mom slow down, turn around, and hold out her hand to her child. It wasn't a coincidence; a real change took place.

How many times could we release the peace Jesus left us to alter our environments? We need to recognize the nudges from the Holy Spirit. Do you walk in peace? Do you know that peace? *Selah.* Peace will guard your heart and mind as you become more aware of it and walk in it. Look at Jesus; nothing rattled Him. He walked and functioned in peace. Be aware that you first must walk in peace before you can release it. Is there a need in your life? Pray, trust God, and let God be God.

I didn't know when my son first moved to California for work that he was living in a friend's closet and had no money. On one occasion when there was no food to be had, he prayed, walked outside, and found a twenty-dollar bill on the sidewalk. He wasn't anxious or worried about his present circumstance because he knew God would always provide for him. *His confidence in God brought him peace.* There are so many other times that I could tell of God's miraculous rescues. It brings joy to my heart to just remember God's faithfulness to me and my family, so remember His faithfulness in your life, and walk in that peaceful confidence.

We have a genuine God who does not want us to worry or be anxious for anything. Commit yourself fully to Him, and He will guard your heart and mind from the enemies of your soul. Ask Him to teach you how to walk in this peaceful confidence. You will notice a difference!

Perfect Peace

> Open the gates, that the [uncompromisingly] righteous nation
> which keeps her faith and her troth [with God] may enter in.
> You will guard him and keep him in perfect and constant peace
> whose mind [both its inclination and its character] is stayed
> on You, because he commits himself to You, leans on You, and
> hopes confidently in You. So trust in the Lord (commit yourself
> to Him, lean on Him, hope confidently in Him) forever; for
> the Lord God is an everlasting Rock [the Rock of Ages).
> —Isaiah 26:2–4 (Amplified Bible)

> Then He arose and rebuked the wind, and said to the sea,
> "Peace, be still!" And the wind ceased and there was a great
> calm. But He said to them, "Why are you so fearful?
> How is it that you have no faith?"
> —Mark 4:39–40 (NKJV)

Perfect peace sustains a restful assurance, even through the most difficult of storms. Peace from God comes when the heart and mind trust Him completely. The natural heart and mind are fickle and jump from one thing to the next, constantly leaning on human understanding and human resources. A heart and mind that stays on Christ securely rests in God's everlasting strength, faithfulness, and resources. Fear, anxiety, doubt, and lack cannot exist in an environment of peace.

The disciples—fishermen who were all too familiar with violent storms and who instinctively responded out of their limited understanding—woke Jesus. Jesus arose, calmed the storm, and turned to them, asking, "Where is your faith?" What a radical statement this must have been to the disciples. May I suggest that Jesus did not intend for them to quiet the natural external storm, but He did want them to quiet their internal storms of fear. Neither Jesus nor His disciples could have gone down with the ship; it was an absolute impossibility. How could a storm kill God? What is wind and rain, personal lack, or life's difficulties, compared to God?

So trust in the Lord, and hope confidently in Him forever. Those around you may be blind to God's grace, but they will see God as you live in peace during the trials and difficulties in your life. If storms are unable to drown you, while joy sustains you and grace continues to strengthen you, then who or what can destroy you? If you possess peace, you can quiet any storm.

Sons of God

Blessed are the peacemakers, for they will be called sons of God.
—Matthew 5:8–10 (NIV)

For I consider that the sufferings of this present time are not worthy to be compared with the glory which shall be revealed in us. For the earnest expectation of the creation eagerly waits for the revealing of the sons of God.
—Romans 8:18–20 (NKJV)

Have the hills, trees, animals, mountains, and all creation really been eagerly waiting for the peacemakers to be revealed? What an amazing revelation to think that creation actually has been waiting for people of peace to *arise* and come into existence. One definition in *Webster's Dictionary* of arise is "to rise from a quiet, inactive, or subjugated state to become active, vocal, or rebellious." Have you ever noticed when you are calm and approach a situation peacefully, problems seem to diminish? Storms rage around us every day at work and in our lives, but they can be silenced. My father never let circumstances unravel him. He was a man of peace, and he always seems to carry a calmness wherever he went. Growing up, there was always an assurance that wisdom and clear direction would come from his advice. He moved in peace, and he deposited peace wherever he went. He was a blessed man and those he dealt with were blessed by just being around him.

No one can make you angry, disturbed, sad, or disappointed; only you can give way to these monsters that want to rob and destroy the peace that is guarding your heart and your mind. Rise above the chaos in your life, and step into this new day as a peacemaker, extending peace to the world around you. Then rest in God's peace and let it fall like rain upon others. All of creation is waiting.

The Lord Is My Shepherd

The LORD is my shepherd; I shall not want. He makes me lie down in green pastures; He leads me beside quiet waters. He restores my soul; He guides me in the paths of righteousness For His name's sake. Even though I walk through the valley of the shadow of death, I fear no evil, for You are with me; Your rod and Your staff, they comfort me. You prepare a table before me in the presence of my enemies; You have anointed my head with oil; My cup overflows. Surely goodness and loving kindness will follow me all the days of my life, and I will dwell in the house of the LORD forever.
—Psalm 23 (NAST)

In such a busy world—with phones, e-mails, text messages, interruptions, appointments, work, friends, family, places to go, people to see, things to do, and hurry, hurry, hurry—*pause*, step back, and reflect on the hectic and sometimes chaotic life you are living. The Lord is your Shepherd, and He will always gently lead. It is the enemy who drives you. Jesus always gently leads you. The Word says, *"Peace, be still and know that I am God"*; rest, trust.

Early morning is my time. With no agenda, I have my morning coffee with the Lord. Sitting alone with Him and meditating on the Word and those I love, with prayers quietly spoken, a peace settles upon my soul, and I begin a new day. This same peace, in the midst of the storms, has carried me throughout my Christian life. Although my humanity tugs and pulls with deliberate attacks of anxiety, the still small voice of the Holy Spirit speaks. Then it is my choice to either listen or to give in to the circumstance.

The Lord's vision, given to me in 2003 about floating in the ocean, is about trust. To float, like trust, demands little physical effort. One simply needs to breathe and lays on top of the water. Isn't it remarkable how relaxed the body is when floating; no anxiety. Trusting God should be like floating. If you are truly seeking the Lord and trying your best to follow Him, then relax, take a deep breath, believe the Lord who loves you, will be faithful to provide and protect you. Lean not on your own understanding and don't resist or struggle, if you do, you'll soon become exhausted and may end up moving away from your destined goal. Look at Jesus, He has the ability to keep you from drowning.

In life, we cannot see where we are going and are not prepared to meet the many challenges before us, but if we learn how to trust God, which I have come to understand as floating, we will go through the deep waters without drowning and will go through the fires without being burned.

The psalmist says, "He makes me lie down in green pastures and gently restores my soul." Withdraw from the hustle and bustle and spend time with God. Let His peace and stillness lead you beside the still waters. Float, let go, and trust God with every facet of your life. Allow His gentle hand to comb through your hair as you rest quietly at His feet, trusting in Him and His promises. Make room today for His peace.

The Shelter of God

The LORD is my shepherd; I shall not be in want. He makes me lie down in green pasture; he leads me beside quiet waters; he restores my soul. He guides me in paths of righteousness for his name's sake. Even though I walk through the valley of the shadow of death, I will fear no evil, for you are with me; your rod and

your staff, they comfort me. You prepare a table before me in the presence of my enemies. You anoint my head with oil; my cup overflows. Surely goodness and love will follow me all the days of my life, and I will dwell in the house of the LORD forever.
—Psalm 23:1–6 (NIV)
A psalm of David

Yesterday as I was in my garden, I was reflecting on still waters. He leads us beside the still waters to restore our souls. What a wonderful place. It is an abiding place, where we can hear His voice in the peaceful stillness. No music, no noise, no running here or there, no stress, no pressure—just a wonderful place where your soul finds rest.

Psalm 91 says, "He who dwells in the shelter of the Most High will rest in the shadow of the Almighty." Both the twenty-third and the ninety-first psalms refer to a place of rest and a place of peace and safety, where your soul (mind, will, and emotions) is quiet, not anxious. Psalm 91:11 goes on to say God has commanded his angels to guard you and to keep you in the palms of their hands so you will not be harmed. In Psalm 91:14, the Lord says He will rescue and protect you as you call upon Him. Do you believe that? *Selah.*

To dwell refers to living within a shelter, similar to a marital relationship. The shelter of the Almighty is a safe place, a place of refuge, where He is living with you. If you remain in that place and draw near to Him, trusting in His ability to help in all circumstances, He will draw near to you.

Sometimes He makes you lie down in order to restore your soul. Willingly surrender and abide with Him, rest, and He will give you peace that passes all understanding, which will guard your heart and your mind. Be still, and let Him lead you beside the quiet waters. *Selah.*

Be blessed today as you wait upon God in the stillness of that shelter. I pray every day that your soul will be restored as you live in Christ.

Note: Psalm 91 was written by Moses. Can you imagine Moses, with thousands of people to feed in the desert, saying, "He is my refuge and my fortress, my God, in whom I trust"? Where did he get the food to feed the people? Where did he get the water? *Selah.*

Chapter 6

GRACE

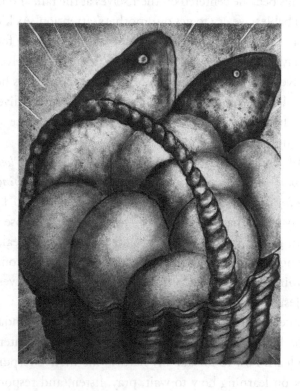

It's all about Jesus, not by your works, Jesus did it all.
Less of me, more of Him
"for the joy set before Him, He endured... consider Him
who endured such opposition..."
Hebrews 12:2-3 (NIV)

> Therefore, my dear friends, as you have always obeyed
> not only in my presence, but now much more in my
> absence—continue to work out your salvation with
> fear and trembling.
> —Philippians 2:12 (NIV)

Human beings became centered on themselves at the fall, and nothing has changed. As babies, we cry to get our mothers' attention. As kids we learn what to do and what not to do. We develop abilities to care for ourselves, protect ourselves, defend ourselves, and make a way for ourselves. We learn how to survive. Then one day the job of managing ourselves becomes too weighty. Problems, responsibilities, and schedules flood our lives and a cry goes out, "Where is God?" In the silence, a still small voice speaks. You can argue, ignore it, respond, or reject it.

In my life, on that day, I thought, *What do I have to lose? Nothing. I don't like how my life is going, and I have failed at everything I've tried, so with nothing to lose, maybe I have something to gain.* So I said, "Yes, come into my life." That was my story—with nothing to lose and maybe something to gain, I gave God a try. I had no idea it was real, but in the days following, God took me through confirmation. He confirmed His reality in unimaginable ways. Once Christ opened my eyes, he put a hunger for Jesus into my heart.

It has taken a lifetime to undo the old established foundation of my life. I have had to work at breaking free from my old self-centeredness and have had to learn how to forsake my natural instinctive responses. I have had to work on learning how to wait, pray, listen, and respond to godly instruction, instead of jumping into situations with my natural human abilities.

I wish I could tell you it has been easy, but I can't, because following Jesus is contrary to human nature. How do we become dependent on the Lord when we have been independent all of our lives? *Selah*. Little by little, bit by bit, with the help of the Holy Spirit, we keep moving forward each day. Talk to Him, ask Him to help you overcome, learn to trust Him, read your Bible, study the Lord's character, and step out in faith. Try to take a walk with Him every day, tell him your problems, share with him your joys, and build a relationship. Slowly but surely, fear, doubt, and self-centeredness will dim as you work out your salvation. Each day you will become less, and He will become more. Keep going, believe, and trust.

Five Types

In reply Jesus said: "A man was going down from Jerusalem to Jericho, when he was attacked by robbers. They stripped him of his clothes, beat him and went away, leaving him half dead. A priest happened to be going down the same road, and when he saw the man, he passed by on the other side. So too, a Levite, when he came to the place and saw him, passed by on the other side. But a Samaritan, as he traveled, came where the man was; and when he saw him, he took pity on him. He went to him and bandaged his wounds, pouring on oil and wine. Then he put the man on his own donkey, brought him to an inn and took care of him. The next day he took out two denarii[a] and gave them to the innkeeper. 'Look after him,' he said, 'and when I return, I will reimburse you for any extra expense you may have.' "Which of these three do you think was a neighbor to the man who fell into the hands of robbers?"
—Luke 10:30–36 (ESV)

Trust in the Lord with all your heart and lean
not on your own understanding.
—Proverbs 3:5 (NIV)

There are five entirely different human mind-sets that affect behavior in the story of the Good Samaritan: (1) the victim who is beaten and left to die, (2) the thief who is self-serving, (3) the priest and (4) the Levite who are prideful and self-righteous, and (5) the Samaritan who showed genuine feelings. All the characters in the story parallel human natures, and all of them can be active in Christians.

- There are those, who, like thieves, rob, steal, and destroy. Whether by word or deed, their actions toward others often are intentionally devastating—an abusive parent, spouse, or employer can kill the hopes or dreams of someone just by simply putting that person in his or her "place."
- The priestly nature honors religion and religious ritualistic ceremonies and doesn't want to be involved. These people look like Christians and act like Christians, but don't live as Christ. They close their ears to the Holy Spirit and only see the selective passages in the Word that support their desires.
- Believers who walk with a Levite character are legalistic in nature with dos and don'ts that they believe will liberate them from acts of kindness toward "questionable" types. In their minds, their belief is the only accurate one, leaving no room for grace. Nonbelievers will run away from this type and will definitely not listen to them.
- Believers with a Samaritan nature look and act like Christ. They give and give and have little thought of their personal needs. They look to Christ throughout their day and seek the Holy Spirit for advice. They trust the Lord and have servants' hearts.
- Sadly enough, the man beaten by the side of the road represents all those who lay waiting for help to come. They are desperately looking for a Savior, not knowing what He looks like but hoping that He will come.

If we are the body of Christ, will we go? Unless believers want to be delivered from the deceptions in their own lives and be as Christ, the lost will continue to go unnoticed.

What drew you to Christ? Was it the ceremonial attractions, or was it that Jesus saw you and bent down to help you? Did He hesitate or worry about getting His hands dirty when He rescued you?

I was that victim lying by the road when Jesus found me. He drew me from my cruel, hopeless pit of despair and saved me. I have had my life restored and delivered from certain death, as have others like me. We gladly give our minds, souls, bodies, and strength to this wonderful Savior. Let us hold on to our great salvation and allow God to use us as instruments to bring healing and deliverance to this world that is littered with the beaten and bruised. Let the Christ in you generously show compassion and offer loving care, as Christ has first shown you.

Good Friday

You will be my witnesses in Jerusalem, and in all Judea and Samaria, and to the ends of the earth.
—Acts 1:8b (NIV)

Halfway around the world, two thousand years ago, three men were crucified, one of whom claimed to be the Son of God. No one knew about it, and no one grieved, except the man's mother and a few friends. Later, news of this event would spread and travel well beyond the territory. This man's story eventually spread, but so what? What difference would it make? People live and die every day. Right?

On this particular Friday morning, a woman began her day, unchanged by the events done in this obscure place so long ago. Who knew? Who cared? It was just another day. The sink was still filled with last night's dishes, the kids still had to get to school, and there was still so much to be done before work. With such a busy schedule, who cared about some man's death and what difference did it make? Why does this death stand out? Why is this man's tragedy any different from other tragedies? Why does this man's death change things? Was it his claim to be God? Were people just preoccupied with this one man's story, or was there really something to his message?

This man talked about a God, a kingdom, and an afterlife. This God was good, and this kingdom was without end. All people who entered this kingdom would be given everlasting life. There would be no cancer, pain, sorrow, trouble, house payments, bills, quarrels, rejection, or death.

But how would the woman know if this man's message was true? Why would she trust some man's story from a different culture, among people she didn't even know? Maybe it sounded good, and perhaps it might tug on the heart, but could it be true? Was there really hope? Were people just kidding themselves or could this be real?

She thought, *This man's story is still being told, and people are being killed every day because of this man. Why?* What if it was true, and this man actually was the Son of God? What if God was real, and what if there was an afterlife without pain, chaos, or problems? She hoped she would get to go there. *I wonder if it's real. I've had pain enough for two lifetimes. This place sounds wonderful.*

After all, her hectic schedule was only getting more complicated, and life hadn't turned out as she dreamed. But how could she find out, who could she ask?

I really have nothing to lose, she thought, *but if it is true, something to gain, maybe I'll ask Bev at work. She seems so nice, and there is something different about her. Maybe she knows something.*

The Heavens

For since the creation of the world God's invisible qualities—his eternal power and divine nature—have been clearly seen, being understood from what has been made, so that men are without excuse.
—Romans 1:20 (NIV)

The heavens are telling of the glory of God; And their expanse is declaring the work of His hands. Day to day pours forth speech and night-to-night reveals knowledge. There is no speech, nor are there

words; Their voice is not heard. Their line has gone out through all the earth, And their utterances to the end of the world. In them He has placed a tent for the sun, Which is as a bridegroom coming out of his chamber; It rejoices as a strong man to run his course. Its rising is from one end of the heavens, and its circuit to the other end of them; and there is nothing hidden from its heat."
—Psalm 19:1–6 (NASB)

As a small child, I would lie on our porch and count stars. My sister, Beverly, and I would find lots of animal and objects in the sky, but we would fall asleep long before we counted all of them.

I imagine that David, in the fields at night, was a stargazer. Night after night, he tended his sheep and likely pondered the stars. No telling how the heavens' beauty and majesty stirred questions in his young mind.

My dad was a builder, so I grew up loving to watch things being made. For me, gazing into the nighttime sky brings me back to my childhood and questions like, how was it all made? Why are there stars? Why are there planets? Why are they all round? Why are they spinning? What combinations of gases were used to make them shine billions of miles away? How big is space? Some people believe that everything we see today was created out of an enormous explosion, but my question is this: where did all that matter come from that caused them to explode? The heavens present all sorts of questions, and the only explanation I can conclude is that there must be a Creator. Then another question arises: if there is a Creator, then why did He create and for what purpose?

The scriptures say it was because God was showing His eternal power and divine nature. What is He like? Without a doubt, he must have unlimited imagination and power. Who is He, and where did He come from? Could I possibly approach such a being? Why would He create us and all the heavens if He didn't want to show Himself and communicate with us in some way?

No matter what language is spoken, the heavens all speak the same language. Scripture says, "The heavens declare the glory of God; the skies proclaim the work of his hands. Day after day they pour forth speech; night after night they reveal knowledge." They have no speech they use no words; no sound is heard from them. Yet their voice goes out into all the earth, their words to the ends of the world" (Psalm 19:1–4 NIV).

God wants His creation to seek Him. He created the heavens so that they would.

I Met a Man

I founded Command Two Ministries in 2003, a ministry based on the Lord's second commandment; love thy neighbor as thyself. Praying for people and being pro-active to respond to real needs, were our main focuses. In September of 2009, I was invited by pastors to come for a week in Uganda and a week in Kenya to teach on prayer and lead nightly revival meetings. Each evening there was to be worship and a message, but on this particular evening, as the Kenyan worship team finished, the Lord down-loaded me with my message. I had told the crowd the night before I would tell them my story, so I did.

I told them that I had been born blind, and my world was filled with darkness. I was always bumping into things and was never able to see the unimaginable beauty surrounding me. I told them of the times when I would trip and fall, most of the time without serious injury, but at times the fall broke my heart and had hurt others. Because I was living in the dark, I had no understanding of the world around me. How could anyone describe the beauty of a sunrise, or the majesty of snow-covered mountain peaks, or a quiet, hidden stream in a lost valley? How could anyone describe what only sight can convey? To see my father's face and to look into his gentle eyes was not possible for me. I could only imagine what he looked like. How different a world of light and sight would be, where colors and texture define every element and where motion differentiates life from death. How beautiful is all of creation for those who have eyes to see, but I was blind.

Along with my blindness, I had been born deaf. I heard no one whisper my name or children laughing. There was only silence in my world of darkness. I only knew what I knew. My scope was very small, with only my mind to paint a world based on my limited reality. Like trying to describe a broken heart, I was unable to define reality. Real light, color, sound, music, and beauty were totally unknown to me. This dark silent world was not of my choosing, but it held me captive. Oh, how I longed to escape and be free.

Then I met a man who touched my eyes so I could see; a man who touched my ears so I could hear. All the warped imaginings faded away in light of His beautiful face. All of creation glistened with colors and beauty too wonderful for words. The voice of my father reached my ears, "I love you," he said as he gazed ever so gently into my eyes. How could it be that such beauty, such love, could have been there without my knowing? My barren world could neither see nor hear until that man touched me.

That man changed my existence. In my dark world, I thought I had been alive, but when he touched me, I realized I had never known real life before, only existence. He gave me life so I no longer would stumble and fall in the darkness and no longer would miss his whispers and the music around me. I could hear every melody throughout all of creation and see every living detail. Oh, how that man changed my life. The man, Jesus, saved me.

I told them my story of how I once was lost, but Jesus rescued me. I once was blind, but Jesus gave me sight. I once was deaf, but Jesus opened my ears to hear. I once was dead but Jesus gave me new life.

Joseph's Story

Then they came to Jericho. As Jesus and his disciples, together with a large crowd, were leaving the city, a blind man, Bartimaeus was sitting by the roadside begging. When he heard that it was Jesus of Nazareth, he began to shout, "Jesus, Son of David, have mercy on me!" Many rebuked him and told him to be quiet, but he shouted all the more, "Son of David, have mercy on me!" Jesus stopped and said, "Call him."

So they called to the blind man, "Cheer up! On your feet! He's calling you." Throwing his cloak aside, he jumped to his feet and came to Jesus. "What do you want me to do for you?" Jesus asked him. The blind man said, "Rabbi, I want to see. "Go," said Jesus, "your faith has healed you." Immediately he received his sight and followed Jesus along the road.
—Mark 10:46–52 (NIV)

And the LORD said, "My Spirit shall not strive
with man forever, for he is indeed flesh."
—Genesis 6:3 (NKJV)

I was preparing to be a counselor for a Billy Graham crusade when my son Joseph asked me what I was doing. I explained to him why people needed to ask Jesus into their lives, and I asked him if he had ever done that. He said no, but someday he would. I said, "What if you were walking home from school, and the driver of a truck lost control, right as you were crossing the street?"

He said, "I would quickly ask Jesus to be my Savior before he hit me."

"What if you didn't have time?" I asked.

Desperate, needy people do desperate things, and in the case of Bartimaeus, he was making a scene. He didn't know if Jesus would ever pass his way again, and he didn't want his only chance to walk by him. He knew he was blind, and maybe if he could get His attention, Jesus might possible bring him sight. What if Bartimaeus had said, "Oh, He's busy. I'm not worthy. I don't want to bother Him," or "Maybe next time"?

The Matrix is a story about people who are programmed and spiritually blind. They think they are living life, but in fact, they are not. As they go through their lives, they try to fix their own problems, solve their own dilemmas, and live their own dreams, totally unaware of their robotic condition. Bartimaeus knew he was blind; there was no illusion.

The Word says that God's Spirit will not always strive with man. We are to seek Him while He can be found. We all have family and friends who are numb and desperately yelling in the matrix of their lives. The Jesus who lives in you walks by them. Are they reaching out? Are you leading them to the one who gives sight to the blind?

My sweet son Joseph went up to his bedroom that day. He came downstairs about thirty minutes later and told me what he had done. Jesus had walked by and stopped at Joseph's bedroom that day, and as my little boy spoke to God as he knelt by his bed, God came into his room and into his heart and opened his eyes.

Laws, Laws, and More Laws

The law is not based on faith.
—Galatians 3:12 (NIV)

So the law was put in charge to lead us to Christ that we might be justified by faith. Now that faith has come, we are no longer under the supervision of the law.
—Galatians 3:24–25 (NIV)

Does God give you his Spirit and work miracles among you because you observe the law, or because you believe what you heard?
—Galatians 3:5 (NIV)

Do not think that I have come to abolish the Law or the Prophets; I have not come to abolish them but to fulfill them.
—Matthew 5:17 (NIV)

Laws, laws, and more laws. Like buzzards waiting to pounce on unsuspecting prey, the scribes and Pharisees intently watched Jesus to find some way to bring Him down. Jesus asked, "Is it lawful on the Sabbath days to do good, or to do evil? To save life, or to destroy it?" (Luke 6:9 KJV). Then Jesus looked around and instructed the man to stretch out his hand. (Mark

3:4–5 KJV) adds that "he looked around at them with anger, and being grieved for the hardness of their hearts," He healed the man.

The scribes and Pharisees lived by the Jewish laws, all 613 of them, a virtual to-do list. The Torah was considered to be the very Word of God, and it never would have occurred to any Jewish person to disobey any portion. It was all they knew. They had become robotic in their obedience to it, so much so, that the law itself bound them. The law had become their religion. No wonder they were oblivious to the Messiah in their midst.

What appealed to the common man about Jesus that they missed? *Selah.* Was it the forgiveness from sin He offered or perhaps the gentle mercy He freely showed? Was it the possibility of freedom from the oppressive rules and regulations, or was it the promise of a better life? I often wonder if our traditions, habits, and worldviews distort us from seeing God. There is saving life in Christ, but man-made dos and don'ts only dilute our ability to tap into God's reality. No wonder Jesus was angry at the leader's stubborn reluctance. Seeing but not believing, they rejected the miracle.

If the scribes and Pharisees knew all the prophecies and promises and were supposed to be looking for the Messiah, why didn't they recognize Jesus? Might it be that religion and/or personal pride blinded them to the possibility of this common Messiah standing before them? Ordinary people who listened to Jesus followed Him in droves, so why were most of the religious leaders unmoved? Did they not see the miracles or hear Him speak? Didn't they ever wonder? Were they genuinely looking for the Messiah, or were they more comfortable with *their* religion and didn't want to change their lifestyle? The question needs to be asked: where are we? *Selah.* It's a matter of the heart. Are we open toward God or closed? Are we going to forfeit God's grace to hold tightly to our religious dos and don'ts? Then what do we do with answered prayer, or the miracles occurring around us, or the Word of God?

The Bible says, "Choose this day who you will serve." The evidence of His reality surrounds us. Ponder the miracle of a newborn baby, the colors in a flower, the many beautiful birds, and all of creation. What about the still small voice in your mind, speaking just at the right time? Will we chalk it up to coincidence, or will we become aware of the fully alive, invisible being speaking to us? Life does not come from nothing. Laws are ink and paper, but Jesus lived, died, and is still fully alive. He gives us living words that speak to our souls—personalized, life-giving freedom.

Temptations of Christ

> Jesus, full of the Holy Spirit, returned from the Jordan and was led by the Spirit in the desert, where for forty days he was tempted by the devil. He ate nothing during those days, and at the end of them he was hungry. The devil said to him, "If you are the Son of God, tell this stone to become bread." Jesus answered, "It is written: 'Man does not live on bread alone.'" The devil led him up to a high place and showed him in an instant all the kingdoms of the world. And he said to him, "I will give you all their authority and splendor, for it has been given to me, and I can give it to anyone I want to. So if you worship me, it will all be yours." Jesus answered, "It is written: 'Worship the Lord your God and serve him only.'" The devil led him to Jerusalem and had him stand on the highest point of the temple. "If you are the Son of God," he said, "throw yourself down from here. For it is written: " 'He will command his angels concerning you to guard you carefully; they will lift you up in their hands, so that you will not strike your foot against a stone.'" Jesus answered, "It says: 'Do not put the Lord your God to the test.' ""When the devil had finished all this tempting, he left him until an opportune time."
> —Luke 4:1–13 (NIV)

In one moment, Jesus is being baptized, the sky opens, and His Father announces, "This is my beloved Son." In the next moment, He is led into the wilderness and tempted for forty days—a definite mountain valley emotional challenge. Jesus would have naturally been hungry, so it is not surprising the devil tempted Him with food, which, by the way, was the original object of temptation. There were stones of flint and limestone on the mountains of Judea that resembled loaves of bread, and Satan tempted Jesus with turning the stones into bread. It wouldn't have been a temptation if Jesus were not able to do it, but the devil tried to get Him to use His miraculous powers to supply his personal need.

Jesus only saw the needs of others, never His own. When He came to earth, He emptied Himself and did not regard equality with God as a thing to be grasped but took the form of a bondservant. Jesus's response, quoting Deuteronomy 8:3, was exactly what Moses had spoken to the Israelites in the wilderness during their forty years. Though Jesus was hungry, He knew the source of His life; it was not bread alone.

The second temptation took place as Satan stood as the pseudo-ruler of the world. The condition was that Jesus bend His knee to the devil. Jesus's response was to quote Deuteronomy 6:13, where Moses warns the people to resist temptation and worship God alone. Although Jesus would have regained world rulership if He had given into temptation, He would have obtained it by depending on Satan, rather than on God. Jesus would not recklessly acquire our salvation through anything short of God's perfect plan.

For the third temptation, Satan took Jesus to the pinnacle of the temple. This was about seven hundred feet above the Kedron Valley or about half as high as the Empire State Building. Satan wanted God to jump off and command His angels to keep Him from smashing on the rocks below. Jesus could have called legions of angels who instantaneously would have come, but that was not God's plan. Jesus would not change the timing of God. He knew He must die on a cross for the sins of the world. Displaying supernatural feats was not the way followers were to believe in or accept Him. He responded with Deuteronomy 6:16, "Do not tempt the Lord thy God."

I often wonder how Jesus stayed in control of every thought and of everything that constantly pulled at Him, never losing His patience and always submitting to His Father. And as I meditate upon it, I have come to conclude it was for us. He saw His church, His bride, the one He loves.

He resisted temptation for us so we may live with Him forever. What an amazing Savior we have.

The Fig Tree

Now learn this lesson from the fig tree: As soon as its twigs get tender and its leaves come out, you know that summer is near. Even so, when you see all these things, you know that it is near, right at the door. I tell you the truth, this generation will certainly not pass away until all these things have happened. Heaven and earth will pass away, but my words will never pass away.
—Matthew 24:32–35 (NIV)

"You will hear of wars and rumors of wars, but see to it that you are not alarmed. Such things must happen, but the end is still to come. Nation will rise against nation, and kingdom against kingdom. There will be famines and earthquakes in various places. All these are the beginning of birth pains. Then you will be handed over to be persecuted and put to death, and you will be hated by all nations because of me. At that time many will turn away from the faith and will betray and hate each other, and many false prophets will appear and deceive many people. Because of the increase of wickedness, the love of most will grow cold."
—Matthew 24:6–12 (NIV)

On May 14, 1948, Israel became a nation. Jesus said that this generation will not pass away until all these things have happened. What generation; what things? The generation that understands that, like the fig tree that awakens in the spring from its dormancy, knows winter is almost over, and time is short. A new season is coming.

Jesus said there would be a time when nation would come against nation, that there would be great famines and earthquakes. He paints a picture of great lawlessness and civil unrest. Nightly, the news broadcasts stories of war and threats of war, bombings and killings, fears of countries teetering on the edge of financial collapse, terrorist attacks, natural disasters, and uprisings. We try not to think about it and try to justify what is going on, but Jesus says we *are* to think about it and know the end is near, maybe right outside the door.

Are you ready? *Selah.* No matter what the timing is, the questions need to be asked: have I loved well and forgiven much? Have I spent time getting to know Jesus and trusting in His mercy? Have I been a doer of the Word or a hearer only? Have I sincerely loved my spouse, children, and friends? Have I reflected Jesus in the world I live in? Have I been faithful and prayed for those around me, and have I spread seeds of loving kindness to others? Have I lived well?

No one knows the date or hour, but we are to be concerned about being ready. We need to understand that the generation that sees these things will not pass away until all that God has said is fulfilled. Jesus told Nicodemus that the working of the Spirit is like the blowing of the wind, and just as our ears hear the wind, our spiritual ears are to hear the voice of the Spirit. Let the Holy Spirit speak to you so your life will be spent wisely. I pray the love of Jesus will shine through you to others while there is still time.

Chapter 7

PRAYER

IF we pray according to His will... Selah
What is His Will? Are you listening?

"do not be anxious about anything..." Selah
Phillipians 4:6-7 (NIV)

> And this is the confidence which we have before Him, that,
> if we ask anything according to His will, He hears us. And if
> we know that He hears us in whatever we ask, we know that
> we have the requests which we have asked from Him.
> —1 John 5:14 (NASB)

Would you give your loved one a good gift or a scorpion? The purpose of gift giving generally is to please or help someone, so of course you'd give a good gift. So why would a loving God, who loves you, not listen to you or give graciously to you? Your Father gives good gifts—ideas, truths, answers, help, and so on. If your heart is pure, and you lean upon Him and listen to Him, why wouldn't He hear and answer your prayers?

I have a friend who had a very verbally abusive husband. Years and years went by, with prayers constantly prayed for this husband and the family but to no avail. Nothing ever changed. One night she asked me to pray and seek God on her behalf. I did and told her what the Lord told me. God said, *"It isn't my fault."*

People are free to choose to walk with God or go their own way. This man, who I suspect was a Christian, had chosen to tear down his wife; he did what he felt like doing. It was not God's fault; it was her husband's fault. He chose to live in disobedience to God and to their marriage vows.

Too often we blame ourselves or God if our prayers go unanswered. We live in a fallen world where human beings live their lives, centered around their own wants and desires; it's human nature. God certainly does not want self-centeredness, but because He created humankind with a free will, He does not intervene or force people to live a life of obedience. If that were the case, people would be little robots that God could program. Her husband was neither a robot nor a faithful husband. Their marriage ended in divorce.

My friend has been healing and has absolutely blossomed. She leaned into God and found her safe place in His presence. So although she went through a terrible valley, God never left her side but carried her through it all. Did God take what was meant for evil and use it for His good? Absolutely. Was it God's will that they get a divorce? Definitely not!

Her heart before and after the divorce stayed centered upon the Lord. She had anger and doubts, but she never lost sight of hope and never stopped praying. God heard the prayers we prayed for our dear friend and answered them. Her anger is disappearing, joy is returning, and her family is becoming less dysfunctional. They still have a way to go, but they're headed in the right direction.

The Lord once told me, "Work with the willing." I cannot move an unmovable person, nor can God. If a person is pliable and willing, miracles can happen. We have an amazing God who is able to do far more than we can ever hope or imagine. If we will ask, He will answer. Continue to pray, and be willing to wait for His answers. Trust Him. He knows your heart and hears your prayers.

Intercessors

Lord, give us a kingdom mentality. Like soldiers fighting, we are fighting every day against unseen forces coming against You and Your purposes. Like in Iraq or Afghanistan, many are killed and/or wounded.

Spiritual soldiers are the same—Lord heal our wounds and let us live to fight another day. Help us continue to move toward the finish line. Protect those on the front lines and give them the understanding that they are more than conquerors. Give them a willingness to step out in faith and to fight the good fight."

Some may say, "Lord, I don't have time." Some may say, "Oh Lord, I can't be effective." Others may say, "I may get hurt or killed." Do our brave men and woman in uniform say, "General, I don't really have time to fight today," or "General, I can't be effective"? Or do they say, "General, if I go out there, I might get hurt or killed"? We are engaging in battle with the King of all kings against the enemy of our souls.

I praise You, Lord, for raising up an army of committed men and women—intercessors—who have moved beyond the excuses and who are defending Your kingdom on earth. Help, protect, and provide for them. Give them strength to stand and courage to fight. When busyness, false humility, or fear engages them, give them eyes to see that they are not fighting against flesh and blood but against principalities, rulers, and evil.

Our minds are the battlefield. Will we fight the excuses and move forward through the obstacles, smoke screens, and futile attempts of Satan, or will we yield to our fleshly will? Help us to say, "I can do all things through Christ, who will strengthen me," even when faced with difficulties. Lord, let your kingdom come. Let your will be done.

Child of God, you signed up for the army when you said, "Here I am Lord. Use me." Battle fear, discouragement, hate, unforgiveness, greed, selfishness—these are characteristics that once held you captive. Will you labor with Christ for righteousness sake?

Do you see the legions of angels? Do you see the hand of God? Will you be victorious? Can you overcome? Do you know that God has everything under His control? Do you understand you're submitting your old nature to Him when you pray, "Not my will, but thy will be done"?

The work is hard and may carry physical dangers, but the benefits of laboring with Christ are eternal and cannot be measured.

My Morning Prayer

This morning in prayer, I saw myself in the middle of the ocean; there were no boats. As I prayed and read Psalm 139, a beautiful peace came over me. Some of you are going into unfamiliar territory. Be encouraged. Remember—*He is there.*

When I am in that ocean, all alone, floating here and there, *Lord, You* are *there.* How will You rescue me, or will I be rescued? I don't know. Should I be fearful? No. *Lord, You are there.* Should I doubt? Are You not the God of Moses who parted the waters? Do You not have a plan and a purpose for my life? Can You not draw something good out of this? Who can question Your ways? Who can tell You how to design Your world or how to mold the clouds? How can I presume to know Your mind? So I float upon the waves, believing and trusting in You.

No ships are around to rescue, you may say, but since when does God require ships to save? God used a fish to bring Jonah to dry land.

Lord, I release my fleshly solutions and welcome your creative supernatural interventions. You want me to live and not to be destroyed. You want my life to be abundant and fully blessed. You want me to see my lonely ocean drifting as a surrendering. Will the ocean expose my unbelief? Will the ocean expose my landlocked faith? Will my want to control, my soulish preservation, my human security, my earthly knowledge, or my ability to walk on land be surrendered when I'm floating? Yes. Will I survive? Who knows but God? Is it His will that I drown? No. Is it His will that I live? Yes. Then abandon the land and jump. Float in His strength, and be moved by His breath. His mighty hands will support me and keep me from sinking.

If I live, I live, but if I perish, I perish. Today, set me apart in the ocean of Your divine reality to drift securely on top of the waves, truly trusting and truly confident of Your presence with me. *Lord, You are there*, and nothing can separate me from You. No height, no depth, no principality, no power, and nothing created or anything yet to be created—nothing! You are God. Lord, You live. So, cast me upon that sea of trust.

Release your reality and float.

Personalized Prayer
(fill in the names of loved ones in the appropriate blank spaces)

Dear heavenly Father,

Pour out Your Spirit and bless our communities with Your love. Lord, help us to live in such a way as to reflect Jesus. I ask for divine connections with those who need a friend, an encouraging word, a prayer, or a blessing.

Lord, let love tear down every argument that sets itself up against the knowledge of our loving God, and break off those things that keep people blind and captive to unbelief. We declare there is eternal life, there is hope, there is a future, and there is a Savior who wants to love, guide, and help every day and in every way. Father, remove the clouds hiding Your glorious light and pierce the darkness. Allow me to reflect love, goodness, mercy and grace to all I encounter. Give deaf ears the ability to hear, blind eyes the ability to see, and dead hearts the ability to be awakened. Keep _____ safe; protect [him, her, them] from the one who desires to destroy [his or her life; their lives]. In Your compassion, Lord, draw _____to Jesus. Amen.

Prayer: Thy Will Be Done

Do not be anxious about anything, but in everything, by prayer
and petition, with thanksgiving, present your requests to God.
—Philippians 4:6 (Berean Study Bible)

For my thoughts are not your thoughts, neither are your ways my ways,
declares the Lord. For as the heavens are higher than the earth, so are
my ways higher than your ways and my thoughts than your thoughts.
—Isaiah 55:8–9 (NIV)

God is faithful to His Word. If He said it, He will do it. God's Word cannot come back void. He created all things through His spoken word, so if God says it, it is done. Too many times our prayers go unanswered because we haven't prayed according to His will. If we are honest with ourselves, we all want answers to achieve our earthly self-centered results. Let's face it: what if God asked you to forgive those who despitefully used you, to bless those who mistreated you, or to love those who hated you?

Would you be willing to do so? Remember it is pride that wants its own way. Prayer often goes against our human nature and human instincts. We are asking for God's will, not ours, to be done on earth as it is in heaven. It says in Isaiah that God's ways are not our ways, and His thoughts are not our thoughts. Ask Jesus to help you know what He wants you to pray, and press into Him. It may take many prayers over many months, but God will answer. Look at Jesus—He endured the cross; a punishment He certainly did not deserve, but He endured, and God's will was done.

How do we know the will of God, and how do we know if God will answer? Why would God want us to pray if He didn't intend to answer? God cannot be manipulated. Scripture is clear; if we pray according to His will, we know He hears us, and if He hears us, we know we will receive that which we have asked. God's Word tells us He answers prayer, but His timing is perfect, so learn to wait upon Him.

He is not as interested in our ease as He is in our ultimate character. Asking Him what His will is in any given circumstance is key. Wait patiently until He shows you, and pray confidently. He hears you and will answer. *He tells you how to pray. He speaks, you agree, you pray, and it is done.*

God is good all the time and will redirect whatever the enemy has intended for evil to be used for our good. Life's trials and challenges are generally a result of human intervention in a fallen world, and it is easier to believe in what we see than what we cannot see, especially if God may or may not be doing what we ask. Disbelief in prayer effectiveness is another core problem. The Bible doesn't say "if you pray"; it says, "Pray." It is not up to us to know how a prayer is answered. It's up to us to pray, and it's God's job to release answers out of His wisdom and omnipotence. Continue to submit and obediently ask, and then trust God to respond according to His will and according to His best resolve.

Timing and Prayer

Do not be anxious about anything, but in everything, by prayer
and petition, with thanksgiving, present your requests to God.
—Philippians 4:6

It has been my observation over the years that people don't approach
prayer confidently, mainly because of unbelief. "How do we know the
will of God, and how do we know if God will answer?" they ask. "What
if He doesn't answer? What if He says no?" These questions cast doubt or
disbelief. Think about it, God would not command us to pray if He did
not intend to answer. *Selah.*

God will respond out of His wisdom and loving nature, working
toward His plan for our good. A good question we all need to ask ourselves
is, "Do I trust God, and do I really want to surrender to His will in my life
and the lives of those I love?"

Pride wants what it wants when it wants it, but God wants His people
to be used effectively for His purposes.

Do you know Him? Do you know He hears you? Then trust Him. His
ways are not easy but are always best. He sees the big picture. He is working
things out for you and a multitude of others, and it would be impossible
to try to unravel the complexity of this maze, to discover His will in every
situation. Just know He is interested in you and will often require you to
wait for answers. Waiting will always require patience and faith.

Learn how to wait. In our microwave world, waiting isn't what our
human nature wants to do, but when we actually learn the art of waiting,
stress and anxiety seems to dim. It is so freeing to lay concerns before Him
without fear or doubt, confidently knowing He is faithful and will answer.

For we do not wrestle against flesh and blood, but against principalities,
against powers, against the rulers of the darkness of this age,
against spiritual hosts of wickedness in the heavenly places.
—Ephesians 6:12 (NKJV)

Behold, I have given you authority to tread on serpents and scorpions,
and over all the power of the enemy, and nothing will injure you.
—Luke 10:19 (NASB)

Evil forces are real, and if they are in countries like Thailand, Africa,
South America, and Central America, they are also in the USA. Do not
look on what you see, but look at the evidences of evil and intercede.
Idolatry, women and children used as sex slaves, human sacrifice, voodoo,
hallucinogenic drugs, and so on are just a few. And just because we cannot
see demons does not mean they don't exist. What keeps people oppressed?
What destroys marriages, the youth, and people's finances? What causes
depression and suicide? What causes disbelief and anti-God movements?
Why is there so much depression and corruption? Why are so many people
hurting and not receiving the care or the parenting they need? What could
be causing people to be so blind to the hope we find in Christ Jesus? We
may say that Satan is doing this, but Satan can only be at one place at a
time. He is not omnipresent.

If we believe in Christ by faith, then we need to believe His Word by
faith. In Luke 9, Jesus called His twelve disciples together and gave them
power and authority over all demons, and in Ephesians 6:12, the Word
says, "For our struggle is not against flesh and blood, but against the rulers,
against the authorities, against the powers of this dark world and against
the spiritual forces of evil in the heavenly realms."_Evil principalities,
powers, rulers of darkness, and spiritual hosts are *real* and very active.

The first thing we need to grasp is the understanding that they do exist.
Then we need to understand that Christ has given us authority to deal with
them. We must pray and use our authority in prayer to fight against the
evil that is bombarding our families, friends, and the world. We do not

fight like the world fights. God has given us the Word as a weapon. It will not come back void but will achieve the very purpose it is sent out to do. Every knee must fall at the name of Jesus, and nothing can come against the blood of Jesus. "The weapons we fight with are not the weapons of the world, on the contrary, they have divine power to demolish strongholds" (2 Corinthians 10:4). Use these spiritual weapons against the evil clawing at your faith, family, health, finances, friends, church, pastor, city, and nation.

Saints of God, it is our job to pray like never before for the unsaved who are bound to the hindering spirit of disbelief; for the sick who are in need of healing; for the oppressed who are in need of deliverance; and for the families and neighbors who are in need of compassion, love, hope, and a future. These same forces that attack our loved ones and neighbors also attack us. Church, arise, and do not be deceived. Your intercession matters and is vital. Someone once wrote, "There is nothing left to do but pray, but there has never been anything else to do but pray."

Who Is Like Our God?

"Which is easier: to say, 'Your sins are forgiven,' or to say,
'Get up and walk'? But so that you may know that the
Son of Man has authority on earth to forgive sins ...
Then he said to the paralytic, "Get up, take your mat and go home."
—Matthew 9:5–6 (NIV)

I pray:

Father, let me rest and meditate and grasp the understanding that I belong to and am loved by You, the only living God. Because Jesus removed all my unrighteousness, I stand before You now, clean, with every mistake and with every sin erased. *Selah.* As I ponder what You have done for me, I ask myself, "Who is like my God?" Who else has ever demonstrated such amazing unconditional love for me or has rescued me from certain death? Who else has covered me with grace or shown me such kindnesses? Who else has healed and saved my soul?

Lord, You are the Creator of all there is, and for reasons I don't understand, You have drawn me into Your kingdom and have adopted me as Your child. You have commanded Your angels to watch over me no matter what I do or where I go. With each new day you lavishly provide me with new mercies. You have promised You will neither leave me nor forsake me and that Your love for me will never fail.

There are not adequate words to tell You how grateful I am, how my heart rejoices that You are a living God who hears me when I pray, holds me when I'm down, and rejoices with me when things in my life are good. I have a hope and a future because with You, all things can be and are possible.

Though the fires rage and the floods come, I will not fear, for You are with me. Your rod and Your staff will comfort me. You go before me, and You follow me all the days of my life, so even though the mountains quake and fall into the seas, I will trust You, for You are my God, worthy of all my praise.

Chapter 8

LOVE

All things are possible for God and God is Love.
Remember then all things are possible through Love.

"God is love." 1 John 4:8 (NIV)

Access into Grace

For the LORD God is a sun and shield: the LORD will give grace and glory: no good thing will he withhold from them that walk uprightly.
—Psalm 84:11 (KJV)

By whom also we have access by faith into this grace wherein we stand, and rejoice in hope of the glory of God.
—Romans 5:2 (KJV)

The Lord illuminates, warms, and sustains life like the sun. He protects and defends all who trust in Him, like a shield in the hands of a mighty man. The Lord gives grace and glory—first grace, as a plant, and then glory, as the fruit. No good thing will be withheld from those who walk uprightly. Our Lord will supply good things but never evil things.

We who believe have been given permanent access into the grace surrounding almighty God, wherein *we stand* and we rejoice in the hope, knowing God's declaration over our lives. As long as we remain walking upright, the shield of God will remain to protect us, the radiance of God will continue to sustain us, and the grace of God will continue to supply our every want and need.

This doesn't mean we will live a life without problems or that every prayer is favorably answered. God is not a genie. He is God, the one who knows our needs before we ask. It does mean, however, that we have access to God's grace and the many grace natures, such as walking without fear, freedom to choose good over evil, the ability to speak encouraging words and to show forgiveness, having the privilege to serve others, and the grace to give our best no matter what we're doing. Do you see how freeing life could be when you understand you have been washed clean and no longer have to live by your old human nature but now can stand before God, clean? *You have been forgiven by grace!* The old is gone; don't ever let it return. You now are free to breath, relax, and live, no longer bound, no longer walking on eggshells in a stress-filled environment.

Grace is God's favor toward the unworthy or undeserving. If you have a job, grace has been given. *Selah.* No one should expect a blessing; it is grace when you receive one. You may say, "But, my boss doesn't appreciate me." Think! Keep your eyes on the reason Jesus wants you there. Maybe, you are to pray for the other employees or be an encouragement to them. Maybe, you are to become the best employee in the company. Maybe, God wants to teach you something to better prepare you for something later. Step back, get a different perspective. The selfish human nature always sees itself. We have been given so much grace. Think of what you do have instead of things you don't. Think of where you once were and where you are now. Why did you get saved? Think on these things…. You can see, taste, feel, and believe; amazing grace!

Amazing Love

> For I am convinced that neither death nor life, neither angels nor demons, neither the present nor the future, nor any powers, neither height nor depth, nor anything else in all creation, will be able to separate us from the love of God that is in Christ Jesus our Lord.
> —Romans 8:38–39 (NIV)

The Bible says that God is love. How do we begin to understand love when we find so little of it in this world? Although our minds cannot grasp, with any understanding, the magnitude of God's love, we do grasp an understanding of human love, based on what we have experienced throughout our lives. The difference between the two, however, is staggering.

In a fallen world, mistreatment, human nature, selfishness, events (good and bad), general goodness and kindness, passions, lust, evil, and so on, all form our picture of love. What we think is love, more often than not, is warped. Because of our twisted worldview of love, most people are unable to differentiate between God's love and human love. People on the outside look at our behavior and associate it with God. People are watching; they see us and hear us every day at home and/or at work. If they see behavior in us that is not Christ like, they may say, "If God looks like those people, I don't want Him." So I contend that if the world could see Christ in us, whether at home or at work, it would be attracted to Him. If the world could see someone who accepts people as they are, who forgives, who unselfishly loves and genuinely cares without motive, the world would notice something different—Christ in us. The following song, "Amazing Love" by Chris Tomlin, says so much. *Selah*.

> Amazing love,
> How can it be?
> That You, my King
> Would die for me?

Jesus showed us what God's love looks like. Try as we might to be Christ like, we fail. But there is good news: *Jesus is alive*, and there is no one He will not love There is no sin He will not forgive, and nothing in all creation will cause Him to leave or forsake us. There is no distance He will not travel; no height or depth He will not reach. His is an amazing love that will go anyplace, anytime, under any circumstance, to rescue us or to be with us. Jesus will not disappoint. He is God, and God never fails. His love is real, trustworthy, and forever.

Nasty Clogs

> And He called the twelve together, and gave them power and
> authority over all demons and to heal diseases. And He sent them
> out to proclaim the kingdom of God and to perform healing.
> —Luke 9:1–2 (NASB)

But He gives a greater grace therefore it says, "GOD IS OPPOSED TO THE PROUD, BUT GIVES GRACE TO THE HUMBLE. Submit therefore to God Resist the devil and he will flee from you. Draw near to God and He will draw near to you, Cleanse your hands, you sinners; and purify your hearts, you double-minded."
—James 4:6–8 (NASB)

This morning I woke up to a clogged drain. A clogged drain must be unclogged before things can get back to normal. As I was praying about this clog, God opened my mind to the nasty clogs that stop and prevent us from living freely.

Clogs prevent spiritual growth. Things like hatred, selfishness, quarreling, anxiety, division, harsh words, hopelessness, manipulation, drunkenness, depression, suicide, addictions, laziness, control, despair and/or lust; all deceptions that can be used to clog our lives. None of these are from God. They exist all around us and will continue to exist until they are put under the feet of Christ. Although they exist, you have been given the authority to cast them out of your life and home, in Jesus's name. These things that come at you are demonic. Christ did not create depression or any other evil-based emotion. Wake up, church, and resist Satan, and he *must flee* from you. God's Word says it, and God does not lie. Take authority over these ugly, grotesque things that are blocking freedom from you, your family, and your home.

Note in James 4:6–8 that *submission comes before resisting.* Tell yourself, "I will submit, Lord, and no longer labor with the enemy by holding on to anything contrary to Your will." Then resist. Live in submission, humbleness, love, forgiveness, trust, faith, and purity. Use practical common sense. Take time to think about what is happening, both physically and spiritually. Be balanced. Choose to do what is right. Be honest. Keep promises. Be courageous in danger and your sufferings, and determine to labor with Christ. When you submit by following God's directives, *then* God will give you the ability to resist the devil. It is hard work, but you can do it. Practice submitting to God every day of your life, and you will develop strong spiritual muscles to resist. Ultimately, one by one, these negative strongholds will be held captive to the obedience of Christ Jesus and will be gone.

In my own life, I had to confess to my husband the anger, bitterness, and unforgiveness I was holding toward him *before* our marriage could be healed. Why hold on to these types of things when they only eat away at you? Step back and honestly look at yourself. Get rid of them, move on, and become who you were meant to be.

Confidence

So do not throw away your confidence; it will be richly
rewarded. You need to persevere so that when you have done
the will of God, you will receive what he has promised.
—Hebrews 10:35–36

Confidence is a characteristic most humans lack, but the Word of God says to have it. In fact, it says, "Do not throw away your confidence, it will be richly rewarded." Hold on to it, so "when you have done the will of God, you may receive what was promised" (Hebrew 10:35–36).

We need to ask the question, confidence in whom? Are we looking at our own ability and finding fault, hindering us from moving forward? Or are we looking at God's ability, the one who is able to do all things. May I suggest that we stop looking at ourselves and look at the God who brought everything into existence? If your faith journey is in response to the Lord's leading, then be confident. He will give you everything you need to succeed, and He is using you to accomplish something good. With that being said, why wouldn't you have confidence? *Selah*. Have you been going your own way?

God looks at the big picture. We, on the other hand, are near-sighted, which disables us from seeing circumstances correctly. When faith is low, confidence is low. Stop looking at the circumstances, and put your faith in God's abilities, so your hope is renewed. You only need to shift gears and redirect your confidence toward God. I know it is difficult to put your faith in an invisible being, but we have come to *know Him* and have history with Him. Draw on His faithfulness toward you in the past. He loves you! Exercise your spiritual muscles, intentionally turn away from the temptation to control or act in your own strength or abilities. Resist doubt and fear, and just talk to Him. Take a walk with Him and pour out your heart to Him. Remember that He knows you and wants the best for you. Trust Him. Remember, the Word says, "to lean not on your own understanding."

He is a big God who knows everything anyway. He shattered all barriers, making Himself available to you anytime and anywhere. He alone is the one who binds up the broken-hearted, sets captives free, and provides for all the needs of those who ask. Let faith arise and get beyond human limitations.

Prayer: Help me, Lord, to know that You hear me. Let my confidence in You increase today as I give You all of my concerns. I want to trust You, Lord.

Maybe things won't turn out according to your plans, but with God free to work in your life, answers will come, and confidence in Him will be strengthened.

Forgiveness

Jesus climbed into a boat and went back across the lake to his own town. Some people brought to him a paralyzed man on a mat. Seeing their faith, Jesus said to the paralyzed man, Be encouraged, my child! Your sins are forgiven. But some of the teachers of religious law said to themselves, That's blasphemy! Does he think he's God? Jesus knew what they were thinking, so he asked them, Why do you have such evil thoughts in your hearts? Is it easier to say 'Your sins are forgiven,' or 'Stand up and walk'? So I will prove to you that the Son of Man has the authority on earth to forgive sins.

Then Jesus turned to the paralyzed man and said, Stand up, pick up your mat, and go home! And the man jumped up and went home! Fear swept through the crowd as they saw this happen. And they praised God for sending a man with such great authority."
—Matthew 9:1–8 (NLT)

How much power is there in forgiveness? Certainly more than enough to accomplish everything Christ was sent to earth to do. When Jesus saw the faith of the paralytic's friends, He forgave the man's sins. The question is, "Is it easier to say, 'Your sins are forgiven,' or 'Stand up and walk'?"

I can forgive someone of his or her sin toward me, but God is the only one who has the power to erase that sin from ever happening. In my flesh, I am unable to heal anyone, but God, with a single word, is able to miraculously restore perfect physical condition. Eyes see, ears hear, the lame walk, dead men live, and the possessed are delivered. It was never a question of healing for Jesus; it was a statement of His authority to forgive.

Through the power of the Holy Spirit, we, too, are used as conduits of God's power, and it is God's power in us that enables us to forgive. Dr. Menninger, founder of the Menninger Clinic, a leading specialty psychiatric hospital and research center, once said that 80 percent of his patients would be fully healed if they would just forgive. Unforgiveness is like pouring acid over yourself and hoping the other person will suffer. It only hurts you! Unforgiveness is like a cancer that gnarls its evil roots into the soul until it takes over. Ask the Holy Spirit to help you to forgive those who have injured you, and let the nail-pierced hands that forgave you bring healing. Forgiveness wasn't easy for Jesus. It took everything He had to establish it—His life.

God Is Love

And so we know and rely on the love God has for us. <u>God is
love.</u> Whoever lives in love lives in God, and God in them.
—1 John 4:16 (NIV)

There is a wonderful God whose name is *love*. His name is wonderful. His
name is protector. His name is provider. He is almighty and He is peace,
mercy, and grace. He is amazing! His love defines me, His Spirit beckons
me, His protection guards me, His provision secures me, His almighty
presence surrounds me, His peace comforts me, His mercy rescues me, and
His grace cleanses me. He is amazing! His name is love. He is the lover of
my heart, the lover of my soul, the lover that beckons me to be His own.
His love lasts forever. He is a lover who knows and sees my potential. He
is the lover who calls me his bride and draws me near. The unfathomable
lover of all time loves me. Love is His name.

In Faith

Yet to all who received him, to those who believed in his
name, he gave the right to become children of God.
—John 1:12 (NIV)

In a world where there are so many options, we should think about what
we will believe or not believe. What is the basis for what you believe? *Selah*.
Is it in a rule book of ways to live, or is it something that has been handed
down to you by others that you are expected to receive and believe?

Something dramatic changed me in the fall of 1975. I can't explain it.
Something happened that logically should not have happened. Somehow
I was awakened to a reality I never knew existed. It wasn't about going

to church, being a good girl, or doing good things; it was different. It had nothing to do with me but had everything to do with Jesus. In my desperation, I had called out to Him, and something happened to me.

He wasn't a statue or historical figure. He was real, alive, an invisible being who was revealing Himself to me. Although I couldn't see Him, I knew He was there. When it dawned on me what had happened, I began to talk to Him, and, miraculously, my life began to fall into place. I had unknowingly received Him, and He was actually confirming His existence to me.

The Bible says that He gives the right to anyone who receives Him to be called His child. What an amazing statement. I didn't have to pay for my unbelief, bad behavior, or rebellion. Jesus did it all. How could this be? How could this one moment make such a difference? Every secret sin— forgiven? How? I wasn't going to be held accountable for my mistakes? How could this be, and why?

It is an impossibility for humans to live perfect lives, lives without negative thought or deeds, so God had to provide a way for them to be in a relationship with Him. Jesus was God's plan. Even though Jesus, being God, had to lay aside His deity to become man, He was exactly that … *man*—the perfect man, with real flesh and bones, the perfect sacrifice for our sins.

Our holy God cannot be in the presence of sinfulness and always required a perfect sacrifice upon which to transfer human sin. It had to be a flawless sacrifice, one that could take away the sins of the people. Never had there been a person who could take on that role, until Jesus.

After my dad died, I went to the funeral home, drowning in grief, to view his body. I prayed, "God, if my dad wasn't saved, take my salvation and give it to him. I'll take his penalty." Through the tears, I heard the Lord say, *"I already did that."* When I heard those words, grief no longer gripped me, and in that instant, I realized I could not have changed places with Dad. Only Jesus could do that. Only Jesus.

I received Jesus in faith. For reasons I do not understand, He took a sinner like me and made me His child. It wasn't about what I had or hadn't done. It is all about Jesus and what He has done. He alone is *Savior*.

Have you received Him? If not, do it now, while there still is time. If you have, then rejoice. You are a child of God.

Love Came to Earth

We have come to know and have believed the love which
God has for us God is love, and the one who abides
in love abides in God, and God abides in him.
—1 John 4:16 (NASB)

Love came to earth and lived among us and became man. Pure love was both the initiator and fulfillment of the perfect redemptive plan to restore what had been lost. Love was flesh and blood without spot or blemish. Love did not find equality with God something to be grasped. Love did nothing apart from the Father's will. Love was unconditional and intentional. Love paid the price for all sins. Love was not boastful or proud. Love was despised and rejected. Love is the most powerful force in the universe. Love will not die. Love always rejoices in the truth. Love never fails. Love bears all things, hopes all things, and endures all things. Love is a choice. Love wins. Love attracts and dwells in the light. Love walks in righteousness.

God is love, and love never fails.
You are so loved. Go, then, and love others.

Love

But I say unto you, love your enemies, bless them that
curse you, do good to them that hate you, and pray for
them which despitefully use you, and persecute you.
—Matthew 5:44 (KJV)

Have you ever been the undeserved target of someone's pent-up anger or bitterness? Where did Saul get the idea David was against him? Was it something David did, or something Saul perceived? Was Saul jealous of David? Did a prideful envy squelch a once-loving relationship?

We live in a fallen world, where we are surrounded by injustices of all kinds, and we can selfishly justify our actions. It is always a challenge when we build close relationships with others because people can neither love us enough nor fill our needs. Life is give-and-take, and Jesus taught us to surrender to love and to be merciful and kind to those who despitefully use us. When wronged, we might say, "I don't deserve to be treated this way," but Jesus didn't deserve to die on a cross. We must constantly surrender our soulish needs to satisfy our flesh for the sake of love.

A kind old man took care of his disabled wife for over sixty-five years. In their life together they endured many difficult circumstances, including the loss of their teenage son. In their old age, neither the difficulties nor the hardships seemed important. The old man lost his memories but continued to remember his wife's loving arms caressing him. Her gentle love and touch brought sweet comfort to his anxiety. It was the language of love that communicated to him, when words no longer could. Love is the most powerful force on the planet and can speak volumes.

Power versus Fear

"The disciples prayed, 'Now, Lord, consider their threats and enable your servants to speak your word with great boldness. Stretch out your hand to heal and perform miraculous signs and wonders through the name of your holy servant Jesus.' After they prayed, the place where they were meeting was shaken. And they were all filled with the Holy Spirit and spoke the word of God boldly."
—Acts 4:19–32 (NIV)

The disciples' greatest desire was to tell the world about Jesus. Their eyes had been opened to the reality of God, and they had witnessed, first-hand, Jesus, as He healed and changed lives forever. Their desire to witness was pure, but they lacked the confidence and the power to bring healing through miracles, signs, and wonders, demonstrating the power of God on earth. Their fervent prayer shook the prayer room, and the Lord heard and answered their prayers and filled them with the Holy Spirit. They were given supernatural power to believe God for all things. Their newfound courage enabled them to overcome all fears. The same Holy Spirit that raised Jesus from the dead was alive in them, and nothing could stop them from speaking of Jesus. Faith had replaced fear.

How many times has fear hindered or prevented believers from speaking boldly about Jesus? It is amazing to me how these men, who were hiding in the upper room one day, became world-changes. The disciples had been radically changed. They had a fresh fire and boldness to courageously leave that upper room and go into the entire world. God had poured His Spirit into them, and they were now willing and eager to face danger, speaking the word of God with a sense of confidence and fearlessness.

If your desire to witness about Jesus is pure, and you pray for more of the Holy Spirit, God will hear and answer that prayer, for that is the will of God. The Holy Spirit lives within each believer, but through life's challenges our human nature has taken over and has pushed the Holy Spirit from His rightful place. Fervently pray for a fresh filling of the Holy Spirit, and allow Him to increase as you decrease. Now, go change your world.

The Choice

"The high priest said to Him, I adjure You by the living God,
that You tell us whether You are the Christ, the Son of God.
Jesus said to him, You have said it yourself; nevertheless, I tell

you, hereafter you will see The son of man sitting at the right
hand of power and coming on the clouds of heaven."
—Matthew 26:63–64 (NASB)

Can you imagine if God separated Himself from you? If He removed His
hand and let you have all the punishment for every error, mistake, sin, idle
word, lie, manipulation, omission, or thought you justifiably deserved?
Can you imagine the lists upon lists of charges against you?

On the night before Christ's death, he prayed, sweating drops like
blood. It was not because He knew He would be beaten, mocked, or spit
upon. It was not because He knew the flogging would rip open a great
portion of his flesh. It was not because He knew men would actually pull
the beard out of His face and strip Him naked. It was not because he
feared the sharp crown of thorns that would pierce His head, and it was
not because He knew soon His hands and feet would be nailed to a cross,
and the excruciating weight of sin would be placed upon Him.

Jesus had never been separated from His Father—ever. The moment
was before Him when His pure heart would be infused with every evil,
from the beginning to the end of time, and His Father's face would turn
from Him and look away. How could He bear that? The anguish of
separation was almost too difficult for Him, so He prayed, "Take this cup
from me." "Do you think I cannot call on my Father, and he will at once
put at my disposal more than twelve legions of angels? But how then would
the Scriptures be fulfilled that say it must happen in this way?" (Matthew
26:53–54).

This was His destiny, His moment in time, and He had the free will
to choose, His need or the Father's plan. He could have asked His Father
for help, and help would have gladly come, but that would have been the
end for us. There was no other Savior waiting in the heavens. There was not
another redemptive plan. There was not another son; there was only one
Savior, one plan, and one Son. That night, He knew the weight was upon
His shoulders and said yes to God and became our sin, separating Himself
from His Father, for us. His love for us stretches beyond measure. He took
all our errors, mistakes, sins, idle words, lies, manipulations, omissions,
and thoughts with Him into death and buried them, once and for all. We
have been forgiven, cleansed by the blood of the lamb. *Selah*.

Two Paths

Finally, brothers, whatever is true, whatever is noble, whatever is right, whatever is pure, whatever is lovely, whatever is admirable—if anything is excellent or praiseworthy—think about such things.
—Philippians 4:8 (NIV)

There are two distinctly different pathways through life. One is based on self-reliance while the other is based on faith. The path based on self-reliance is solely lived around human control and independent decision making. From infancy, we learn how to make choices and solve problems that arise in our lives. These situations and problems require solutions that decide the course of action we take. Wrong choices eventually break down human confidence and leave stress and anxiety, which ultimately produces insecurity and self-doubt. This human pathway is difficult but may seem easier just because it is based on learned behaviors.

The other path is difficult but in a different way. This path requires blind faith. It perhaps seems more challenging simply because there is no prior training, and it totally goes against our preconditioning. Trusting God to guide *is* totally unnatural. Worldly influences invade our minds, moment by moment, and we subconsciously make choices. Those seeking to live by faith must become aware of the things that influence their lives and their surroundings and learn to trade their human instinctive responses for Christ like responses. To live as Christ lived, following biblical principles, takes a yielded soul. To those who yield, God will obligate Himself to keep His promises.

Decide which path you will take, and ask the Holy Spirit to help you. Taking thoughts captive and becoming more aware of your responses and behaviors is difficult because you are human, so practice and pray for the strength of the Lord to help you. Ask that the eyes of your understanding will be opened, and watch how God opens your sight to the many things previously missed. Begin each day with the Lord, and release your cares upon Him. The Bible says, "If He is for you, who could be against you," and "With God all things are possible." Find other promises in scripture and hide them in your heart. Decide this day the path you will take and diligently exercise your spiritual faith. Exercise your mind by meditating on what is true. Seek truth in scripture, and choose to do what is right in God's eyes. Don't trust yourself. *"The human heart is the most deceitful of all things, and desperately wicked. Who really knows how bad it is?"* (Jeremiah 17:9, emphasis added). Humans, by nature, always will protect their own interests and make decisions in their own favor. Jesus did not live according to His will. He did nothing apart from the Father's will. He prayed, "Father, if it is possible, may this cup be taken from me. Yet not as I will, but as you will" (Matthew 26:39).

Remember that God is love, and a loving attitude is always admirable and praiseworthy. While others may not see it and may even reject it, your Father in heaven will be well pleased. I like to close my eyes and see myself standing before God, answering for how I am handling a situation. Will I react in the way of the world or in a Christ like manner? Will loving the Lord be my motivation? Will I act according to God's standards? If I think on such things, it always leads me to the godly solution I'm seeking.

What Sin?

Therefore, if anyone is in Christ, he is a new creation; old things
have passed away; behold, all things have become new.
—2 Corinthians 5:16–18 (NKJV)

The old is gone and the new is before us. Yesterday and last year are both behind us. Old things have died, ended, are no more, no longer exist. It is a new day, a new chance, a fresh start, a miraculous opportunity to begin again. During the depths of our troubles, how we long to leave the old and embrace the new. How can we do that? How can I stop caring for those old friends or stop living my old way of life? Do I just ignore my responsibilities? How do I leave the past behind? If you truly seek a new life, you may have to seek new friends and loftier goals.

The Bible says we all will have troubles, *but* we can approach them with a new empowered mind-set. Look at the beatitudes found in Matthew 5:1–12. God's ways are not our ways. Jesus said to love, not hate; forgive, not seek revenge; be merciful, and not seek retribution.

Our natural tendencies are human and are developed over time by circumstances and environment, so our natural ways of handling life is from our human nature. But now, as a new creation, we have the freedom to act either from our human nature or our new nature. We can approach life deliberately and purposefully. If you are born again, the new nature is within you. With God's help, you can overcome anything; you can make healthy decisions.

The devil comes in to kill, steal, and destroy, and he definitely desires you to live as you have in the past. Don't allow him that authority; don't be imprisoned again. Choose to live as Christ. You are a new creature; all things are new. This new life is of God, and though temptations may surround you, the power of God in you has the ability to overcome anything. You are reconciled with God. You are loved and forgiven, and you are an ambassador of God in Christ's stead. You do not have to respond as you have in the past. Try approaching your circumstances as Christ would have. I love the expression, "What would Christ do?" It comes down to that. The Holy Spirit within you can give you the courage and the peace to be strong in your new nature. That old nature is gone!

I love the freshly fallen snow and how those magnificent soft flakes lay upon the evergreens. You are God's beautiful masterpiece, and just as the fresh-fallen snow glistens, so do you. Remember you have been saved by grace. The old is gone, and the new has come. Let the fresh snow of grace laying upon your life glisten in the light of Jesus wherever you go.

> Finally, all of you, be like-minded, be sympathetic, love one
> another, be compassionate and humble. Do not repay evil with
> evil or insult with insult. On the contrary, repay evil with blessing,
> because to this you were called so that you may inherit a blessing.
> —1 Peter 3:8–9 (NIV)

For the eyes of the Lord are on the righteous and his ears are attentive to
their prayer, but the face of the Lord is against those who do evil. Who
is going to harm you if you are eager to do good? But even if you should
suffer for what is right, you are blessed. Do not fear their threats; do
not be frightened. But in your hearts revere Christ as Lord. Always be
prepared to give an answer to everyone who asks you to give the reason
for the hope that you have. But do this with gentleness and respect.
—1 Peter 3:12–15 (NIV)

When no one else sees, God sees. When I was a child, I would hide
under my blanket, thinking no one could see me. Childish thoughts are
innocent, but when we move from childhood into adulthood, innocent
misunderstandings need to fade in the light of the truth. The Lord sees all
things and is against all those who do evil, so who is going to harm you if
you are eager to do good? The Lord is your rampart and your shield; He
is the lifter of your head and the guard around you. His rod and staff will
comfort you. He goes before you and follows you all the days of your life.
What good thing will He withhold from those He loves?

Good things in God's eyes are different from good things in the
world's eyes. Everything you see originally was created good, but when sin
distorted the elements of creation, humanistic brainwashing distorted our
minds. Are we walking in love, being merciful, and showing grace? Are we
forgiving as we have been forgiven, exercising humility, preferring others
over ourselves, doing good and not harboring anger or bitterness in our
hearts? Are we demonstrating Christlikeness? A lifestyle of these behaviors
will domino—blessing after blessing, joy after joy.

Do you want what God wants? Which reality are you looking at—the reality of the kingdom of God or the reality of this world? God is interested in your character. He is honing a bride for His Son. Are life's difficulties increasing your spiritual strength and faith? Are you traveling on the road less traveled? Are you making tough decisions and resisting compromise with worldly ways? Is loving God and others the foremost thrust in your life? Is the world (from under the blanket) the world you perceive?

Be prepared to give the reason for the hope you have to everyone who asks.

Your Best

For it is God who works in you to will and to
act according to his good purpose.
Philippians 2:13 (NIV)

This morning I was listening to a wonderful song by John Michael Talbot called "Saint Theresa's Prayer."

Christ has no body now but yours
No hands, no feet on earth but yours
Yours are the eyes in which He looks
Compassion on this world
Yours are the feet with which He walks
To do good
Yours are the hands with which he blesses
All the world
Yours are the hands
Yours are the feet
Yours are the eyes
You are His body

When I first realized my work was my ministry, my focus changed. It was more important to be excellent in every detail of my work and offer the best interior designs and not just do ordinary. My attention to excellence built a reputation that opened doors to new people who needed what I had to offer. Relationships grew, and more opportunities opened to me. As I loved and served people, divine appointments began happening. My work availed more than just a fun way to make a living. It also offered opportunities to witness, opportunities to show God's love, and opportunities to exercise God's creative nature within me. People listened and respected what I had to say, and it no longer mattered if I planted the seed, watered the seed, or reaped the fruit. Every step along the way was important because my clients were important. People were important! I saw them as God's human masterpieces, all loved by God—an entirely different perspective than I originally had.

Let the love of God open your eyes to those around you. Open your soul (mind, will, and emotions) to be empowered with Christ's love for everyone with whom you deal, and then offer your best in everything you do. Be God's hands and feet to love others as you first have been loved.

Chapter 9

TRUST

When there are no answers, when your world seems out of control, Trust

... "Lean not on your understanding..." Selah
Proverbs 3:5 (NIV)

> That is why, for Christ's sake, I delight in weaknesses,
> in insults, in hardships, in persecutions, in difficulties.
> For when I am weak, then I am strong."
> —2 Corinthians 12:10 (NIV)

Have you ever been at a place in your life where you can't think? A place where questions outweigh answers? A place that seems hollow and like a void, where your voice is the only one you hear?

Many have survived trial after trial and somehow have managed to continue to move forward. If given the choice, no one would choose hardship. People hate change, and we, as humans, naturally want non-stressful lives, where circumstance bends in our favor. Jesus told us we would have troubles, so for believers, it is when we are weak, vulnerable, and tender that God actively molds and shapes our characters. If we surrender our stubborn, self-centered wills, our mind-set will change. The mind perplexed without understanding will yield to trust. The will, loosed from worldly perceived glamour, will hang on to Christ alone for its only source of strength. Shattered emotions will desperately become dependent on the love and reality of God.

Jesus walked from the garden, deserted by his followers, to the scourging post and then on to the cross and into hell, before returning to His eternal heavenly home. By nature, humans generally are not willing to endure the scourging and do not want their souls to be crucified. But it is only through the scourging and crucifixion of the will that our souls are broken, and we finally say, "Yet not my will, but yours be done" (Luke 22:42).

Those who journey this road will think they have been forsaken by God and those around them, when, in fact, the opposite is true. Under the extreme pressure, they are being drawn closer to God, and their characters are being radically changed.

Continue to stand, continue to trust, and look to Jesus, who is your defense and your protection. Jesus moved through it all, step by step, and so will you, by God's grace.

Be Steadfast and Be Not Afraid

My prayer:

Be gracious unto me, oh Lord, and keep me safe. Help me to follow You all of my days. You, oh Lord, are my strength and my shield in times of trouble. Where else can I go? Who else has the words of eternal life? Who else can grant me peace? Not the peace this world offers but the peace that guards my heart and mind. The peace that keeps me calm in the midst of storms.

You, Lord Almighty, are my only hope. Where else can I run where troubles cannot find me? Who else can I believe? Help me to remember Your faithfulness in the storms that have passed. Let me have faith to believe and eyes to see that Christ is my only true strength. Lend me Your ear, Lord, and hear the cries of my heart. Let my prayers be honest laments from the depths of my innermost being. Do not take Your Holy Spirit from me, but restore my soul and lead me upon the path of righteousness for Jesus's sake.

Let truth come from my mouth, and may my heart never be against Your standards. You are God, and there is none like You. You formed all of the heavens and the earth. You created everything that has been created, and there is nothing seen or unseen that You have not created. In all of creation, there is none like You. You are my God, and You have no equal. I will put my trust in You.

With a breath You blew the waters into place, and made the high places land, and made the low places to be filled. Great are the numbers of the stars, oh Lord. You created them all. You hung them into space and established patterns in the sky to help us navigate. You directed the winds and air patterns to flow, providing seasons of change. You are good, and You have shown me Your tender mercies and have crowned me with Your loving kindness. Help me to cast off my self-imposed sufferings and selfish ways. Why do I compete with others? Am I depending on myself and my strengths to give me confidence? Am I so distant that You cannot work in me, or is my heart hardened and unshapeable? Deliver me from evil and free me from my wicked ways. You stand at the door knocking. God, help me to open the door! Change my heart, oh God, and renew a right spirit within me. Father, not my will, but Your will be done.

Help me to love and not hate, heal and not hurt, bind up and not tear down, build and not destroy. Grant me mercy that I may obtain mercy, grace that I may extend grace, and kindness that I know what kindness is.

Teach me, oh God, and let me see outside my worldview. Open my eyes that I may see through the eyes of Christ and allow me to walk humbly with You, all the days of my life. Help me to work with others, seeking always the kingdom of God and Your righteousness. Help me to trust You, oh God! Help me to stand in the heat of the battles and not faint. Help me to hold on to the grace that holds me together, and help me show love toward others that they too may experience Your tender mercies and loving kindness. You, oh Lord, are my strength. I will not be afraid. In Jesus's name, I pray.

Despair

Trust in the Lord with all your heart; do not depend
on your own understanding. Seek his will in all you
do, and he will show you which path to take.
—Proverbs 3:5–6 (NLT)

It Is Well with My Soul
When peace, like a river, attendeth my way,
When sorrows like sea billows roll;
Whatever my lot, Thou has taught me to say,
It is well, it is well with my soul.

Though Satan should buffet, though trials should come,
Let this blest assurance control,
That Christ has regarded my helpless estate,
And hath shed His own blood for my soul. ...

But, Lord, 'tis for Thee, for Thy coming we wait,
The sky, not the grave, is our goal;
Oh, trump of the angel! Oh, voice of the Lord!
Blessed hope, blessed rest of my soul!

And Lord, haste the day when my faith shall be sight,
The clouds be rolled back as a scroll;
The trump shall resound, and the Lord shall descend,
Even so, it is well with my soul.
—Horatio G. Spafford, 1873

No matter what my lot, God alone has taught me to say, "It is well with my soul." Your soul may still hurt, and tears may still come. Just know you are not alone. Everything might be collapsing around you, but remember the Lord is in control, and He is able to make a way where there seems to be no way; you just can't see it. Keep your mind fixed upon Jesus, your Savior, and pray. Press into Him, and seek Him in every aspect of your life.

Warning: Self-sufficiency and self-confidence have been the ruin of humankind ever since the fall. Man's sin has been to live independently and without God in this world.

Desperate

An angel from heaven appeared to him and strengthened him. And being in anguish, he prayed more earnestly, and his sweat was like drops of blood falling to the ground. When he rose from prayer and went back to the disciples, he found them asleep, exhausted from sorrow.
—Luke 22: 43–45 (NIV)

Life is hard, and at times our world seems to be whirling out of control. Each day seems to bring another hurdle. During a particularly hard season in my life, I anguished to no avail, or so it seemed. If it had not been for the strength of the Holy Spirit in my life, I would not have survived. My personal agony was, at times, more than I could bear. Second by second, I found myself praying for a little more strength, a little more strength—begging for the cup of affliction to be lifted. Jesus too asked for His cup to be lifted.

When these seasons come, remember you are not alone. God is faithfulness, even if things get worse. Jesus had to endure the cross. If you are battling pain, sickness, old age, rebellious children, marriage issues, or simply everyday life challenges, you are in company with Jesus.

> The LORD is near to the brokenhearted And saves those who are crushed in spirit. Many are the afflictions of the righteous: but the LORD delivers him out of them ALL.
> —Psalm 34:18–19 (NASB, emphasis added)

The twenty-third psalm promises that even though you walk through the valley of the shadow of death, you should not fear evil, for God is with you. Everyone has seasons of afflictions, but God promises He will be with us, so hold on to that promise. When a hailstorm is pounding hard outside, as long as you remain inside, you will be protected.

The Word says to lean not on your own understanding—My ways are not your ways. It is so difficult to oppose your human nature, but yielding to God, out of love for Him, will activate His greater purposes for your life to be accomplished. He is working something out, far greater than you can imagine. Love Jesus more, and choose to deal with things as Christ did. More of Christ, less of you. Resist the temptation to use your human abilities to bring godly resolve; flawed humans only bring flawed results. I once heard a pastor say, "God is not as concerned with our circumstances as He is with our character."

I often think of Jesus hanging on His cross, with mankind's sins weighing upon Him. Then my sins are added, making His pain all the more. It makes me cry to think that it was because of my sinfulness He was afflicted, yet that same cross brings me encouragement because if He could go through the pain and suffering of the cross, so can I. His ways are so much higher than ours. Yield, out of love for Christ, and allow the hands of Jesus to use that which the enemy intended for bad to be used for your good. Labor with Christ alone.

Great Is Your Faithfulness

"The steadfast love of the Lord never ceases; his mercies never come to an end; they are new every morning; great is your faithfulness. The Lord is my portion," says my soul, "therefore I will hope in him."
—Lamentations 3:22–24 (ESV)

When you pass through the waters, I will be with you;
and when you pass through the rivers, they will not sweep
over you. When you walk through the fire, you will not
be burned; the flames will not set you ablaze.
—Isaiah 43:2 (NIV)

When I can't remember as I used to do, I must draw on the deep wells that have been established within me. The Lord has been faithful and has always given me the words I need to say, exactly when they need to be said. When I'm alone, I drink from the streams deep within, and I feast on the wealth of understanding that comes with age and experience.

Almost thirty years ago, I desperately wanted to leave the business world and go into full-time ministry, but that door was never opened. I continued working in the marketplace, and forty years later, I asked, "Lord, what is my purpose? Why, when years ago I could have done something of value?" Then I heard God say, *"You weren't ready."* You see, I hadn't walked through the valley of despair or suffering; the valley of tears, doubt, or questioning, some thirty years ago. I couldn't relate with the elderly, or the issue of dementia or Alzheimer's disease, or the loss of friends. I couldn't relate with the valley of resentment when my life flipped upside down. I couldn't relate to those who had lost their businesses or health, and I didn't know what it was like to be handicapped. I hadn't experience the death of two brothers, both parents, and pets or the pain of that loss and separation.

To live a life filled with the physical, mental, and spiritual challenges I have lived through was not the life I anticipated when I prayed, "Whatever you want me to do and where ever you want me to go Lord …"

In the fall of 2003, the Lord told me he was going to take me places where I did not want to go and have me go through things I did not want to go through. A few weeks later, He gave me a vision, along with an interpretation of that vision. I saw myself floating alone in the ocean. I couldn't stand, and I didn't know which way to swim. Then He said to me, *"So you have to trust me."* I had to learn how to float.

Over the past fourteen years, I have become acquainted with pain in every area of my life, and through all those valleys, I have seen God. I remember saying to my pastor's wife when my husband's heart was failing, "I get to see God!" Instead of drowning in desperation and fear during these past years, I have learned to stand upon God's faithfulness. I have witnessed His help and comfort toward me, over and over again. It has transformed my thinking, where I can now say, "I identify with Isaiah 43:2, who said, when I pass through those deep waters, I will not be swept away and when I walk through those fire, I will not be burned."

I'll always remember the vision He gave me in 2003, when He said, *"Trust Me."* I have trusted Him and will continue to do so. I have survived on that Word, hidden deep in my heart, for all these years; it has sustained me. I know His faithfulness will continue to carry me all the days of my life, until I dwell in His house with Him forever.

> Jesus wept.
> —John 11:35 (NIV)

> Blessed are those who mourn, for they will be comforted.
> —Matthew 5:4 (NIV)

How can anyone cope with the loss of a child? In 1864, Mrs. Lydia Bixby received a letter from President Abraham Lincoln, expressing his sadness over the loss of her *five* sons.

Lincoln wrote, "I pray that our Heavenly Father may assuage the anguish of your bereavement, and leave you only the cherished memory of the loved and lost, and the solemn pride that must be yours, to have laid so costly a sacrifice upon the altar of Freedom." (Lincoln's letter to Mrs. Bixby, 1864) Wonderful words of compassion truly express Lincoln's heartfelt sadness, yet they only are wonderful words.

Horatio Spafford, author of the great hymn "It Is Well with My Soul," and Mrs. Spafford lost their four daughters in a tragic sea accident. The words of this father/songwriter testify of something that defies human understanding, called peace. This world can only offer beautiful words that bring little solace to hurting hearts, but for those who trust in the Lord, God's protective peace supernaturally covers and gives inner strength amid the suffering. God tenderly holds the hurting next to His heart. It is in this secret place, next to His heart, where peace is found.

When my brother died at the tender age of sixteen, I experienced and witnessed grief for the first time in my young life. The loss of my big brother was absolutely horrible, and it is beyond my comprehension to imagine death multiplied by four or five. To me, it could only be described as unbearable anguish. The physical death of a loved one is not the only loss that ravages. The death of a marriage, business, personal hopes and dreams, close relationships, a future, and so on implode lives as well. The Word says that Jesus draws close to the brokenhearted and tenderly holds them, weeping with them.

The songwriter says that peace is like a river. When tragedy interrupts lives and grief hits, the world of the survivors becomes dark, lost, and depressed, and only God has the power to deliver them from that pit. A river of peace begins to flood the banks of grief and flows ever so gently through the jagged rocks. The Word says it is only our compassionate, loving Lord who can give us a peace that transcends all understanding. He feels the pain of those who mourn and promises to always comfort them. Trust Him.

He Identifies with Us

He is despised and rejected by men, A Man of sorrows and
acquainted with grief. And we hid, as it were, our faces from
Him; He was despised, and we did not esteem Him.
—Isaiah 53:3 (NKJV)

"You yourselves are a case study of what he does. At one time you all
had your backs turned to God, thinking rebellious thoughts of him,
giving him trouble every chance you got. But now, by giving himself
completely at the Cross, actually dying for you, Christ brought you over
to God's side and put your lives together, whole and holy in his presence.
You don't walk away from a gift like that! You stay grounded
and steady in that bond of trust, constantly tuned in to the
Message, careful not to be distracted or diverted. There is no
other Message—just this one. Every creature under heaven gets
this same Message. I, Paul, am a messenger of this Message."
—Colossians 1:21–23 (*The Message*)

My thoughts of Jesus on that final night of His life on earth bring pain. He was betrayed, beaten, despised, oppressed, rejected, abandoned, pierced, spat upon, scourged, and crucified. Is there anyone with whom He cannot identify?

Often the world presses in, and there is a real sense that life's difficulties are insurmountable. The bombardment of responsibilities, stress, anxiety, and worry invade our lives. I do not read anywhere in scripture where Jesus was worried, stressed, or anxious, but being truly submitted to the Father's will, day by day, He continually moved forward to fulfill His purpose.

When I think of Jesus, I am dumbfounded by His ability to be purposefully focused. We all have been through difficult times in our lives, and even at the breaking point, when the outside pressures were closing in, was there an awareness that it was Jesus the Savior who walked beside you? Did you stress out, or did you realize the purpose and meaning behind your trial? Are we brought through these trials in order that we too might identify with and draw near to those with like problems? Certainly God is working on our characters, but He also is concerned about others and may need you to walk beside them. The trials we experience will tenderize and transform our awareness and sensitivity. Because we can then identify with others who bear the same problem, we can effectively walk with them. Jesus walked in our shoes, and perhaps He wants to assign you to help someone. Prayers and loving kindness will flow from a tenderized heart, becoming a Jesus with skin on to others. Hurting people always respond to those who have walked in their shoes.

Lord, help me to identify with others and bring them the comfort You have shown me. Give me strength to get through every day with joy so I can show love and kindness to those around me.

Jesus Cries for Us

My prayer:

Jesus, you shed tears for us. You made us and had a plan and purpose for each of us. Your will was that none of us would perish, but all would have eternal life. But then sin came into the world, and humankind was captured by evil, looked away, and lost sight of You. How it must grieve Your heart to know we have lost our way and are being held in captivity by such a cruel enemy. How You wanted us to be free to live, love, and walk with You in Your kingdom here on earth.

You know firsthand the evil in this world. You have had your beard pulled from Your face, Your back torn and pierced with straps of metal, and Your hands and feet nailed to a cross. You know the cruelty of humans. How deeply You must feel for us when You see the pain and sorrow we go through, when all along there was a better plan.

Thank you for identifying with our hardships, joys, and sorrows, and thank you for providing the spiritual rescue we so desperately need. Thank you for that hedge of protection that surrounds us and the provision You supply. I will trust You today for Your protection and provision. You are my Savior and my God, the only one who can pull me into that quiet place and restore peace in my heart. I love You.

Learn from Trials

Train up a child in the way he should go; even when he is old
he will not depart from it.
—Proverbs 22:6 (ESV)

No human is exempt from trials or adversity in his or her life, and although the experiences may not be pleasant, most of the time we survive. As humans, we enter this world as self-seekers, blind to God and His ways. Our entire pre-salvation life consisted of selfish wants and desires. Our human nature neither wanted to be less in control nor desired to become righteous. Humans, by nature, establish what and where they want to go and set goals to accomplish it.

The process of becoming Christ like requires a change from a human nature to a godly nature. As children, we all fell many times before we walked. The learning stages God uses, although similar, are different from that of this world. He will use trials to shape us spiritually. Difficult times create dependency upon His ability, His strength, and His faithfulness. Patience is learned by becoming patient, and character is developed, not obtained. Stamina is learned by perseverance, and dependence upon God is achieved through much yielding. Submitting to God and yielding to His will are godly traits.

When I was relearning how to walk after my knee replacement, the physical exercises were horribly painful. Day after day, I forced myself to move muscles and joints that had been traumatized. Every day I had to exercise the knee joint and surrounding muscles so they wouldn't freeze. Finally, the day came when movement became easier. The knee was restored, and I was able to walk again. Developing a spirit of saying yes to God and no to your human nature is very difficult at first, but through endurance the godly nature will begin to emerge.

Olympic athletes train long and hard to master their skills. Their training requires sacrifice and discipline. It is painful to go through trials that grip the soul and grieve the heart, but when they're over, we know we have been changed. It's not a human nature that can react differently to cruelty or hardship and behave as Christ. To love those who persecute, offend, or misjudge us and have the strength and ability to forgive, be kind and to show mercy to them, requires a Godly nature. Disciplining oneself to yield to the ways of Christ, is a day to day and sometimes an hour to hour decision. It requires the relinquishing of natural tendencies to please ourselves for a greater desire to please Christ. Is our love for Jesus stronger than our human need for personal justice? Is our desire to live for Jesus greater than our need to live for ourselves? *Selah* There must be a change of heart, "More of You, less of me."

Being born into the kingdom of God is only the beginning, and like the highly skilled athlete, working out our salvation daily needs sacrifice and discipline. Going against normal human nature and established habits takes perseverance and a disciplined mind-set that agrees with God. Be strengthened with prayer, and persevere to live as Christ. As you mature, laboring with Christ will become more natural. It is not easy—the lessons are hard—but if you let Him, God will strengthen you and will finish what He has started in you.

Psalm 61

My prayer:

Oh God, save me. The floods are rising higher and higher, I sink in the mire; water is all around me. I have wept until I am exhausted. My throat is dry and hoarse, and my eyes are swollen with weeping, waiting for my God to act. But I keep on praying to You, Lord. Pull me out of this mire. Don't let me sink deeper. Rescue me from the deep waters I am in.

God, You know how stupid and self-centered I act. You know all my sins. Don't let me be a stumbling block to those who trust in You. Don't let me cause them to be confused.

How they scoff and mock me when I mourn and fast before the Lord.

Now answer my prayers, and rescue me as You promised. Now is the time You are bending down to hear. I praise God with my singing, and my thanks will be His praise. For my God hears the cries of His needy ones, and He is ready with a plentiful supply of love and kindness.

Resurrection Encounter

Now that same day two of them were going to a village called Emmaus, about seven miles[a] from Jerusalem. They were talking with each other about everything that had happened. As they talked and

discussed these things with each other, Jesus himself came up and walked along with them; but they were kept from recognizing him.
Luke 24:13–16 (NIV)

We only need to go through great grief, adversity, or oppression to know the enormous, hollow heartbreak of shattered dreams and dark tunnels. The Jews had lived for over a century with the nightmare of Roman oppression when Jesus emerged into history. Could this generation of Jews dare to hope that Jesus was really the Messiah? Could they actually put their faith in this Jesus of Nazareth to bring their deliverance from earthly oppression? During Christ's brief ministry, the Jews heard His teachings, witnessed amazing miracles, and had their hearts quickened by His great wisdom. Laying caution aside, they allowed themselves to believe.

Two such nameless men were walking on a road, totally perplexed on how the events of the recent days could have happened. How could this happen if Jesus was the Messiah, the one Jehovah would send to deliver them? Dismayed, sad, perplexed, and somewhat forsaken, these two men were joined by another whom they did not know. To them, Jesus was dead, so no matter how the stranger looked or what He said, their limited minds could not comprehend. Their disappointment was so great that they might not have looked into His eyes. Their shattered hearts only listened to the stranger's words but could not comprehend them. Overflowing with their grief, smashed hope, and a sense of loss, their hearts yearned for a reversal. Just the thought of seeing Jesus alive was beyond their greatest hope and would have defied every bit of human logic.

Night fell, and as they sat and broke bread, something familiar clicked. *Have we not heard this? How could this be?* "Were not our hearts burning within us while he talked with us on the road and opened the Scriptures to us?" (Luke 24:32).

A recognition, a light came on. A shutter flashed, an image became clear, and *poof*! He was gone. With only this one resurrection encounter, joy was refueled and hope became irreversible faith.

In our darkest moments, we do not see or comprehend clearly. Lord, give us a resurrection encounter that opens our eyes and changes our lives forever to the risen Savior right beside us.

> For we wrestle not against flesh and blood, but against
> principalities, against powers, against the rulers of the darkness
> of this world, against spiritual wickedness in heavenly places.
> Ephesians 6:12 (KJV)

Fear is one of the most destructive enemies. It will twist you inside and out with its friend, *anxiety*. It will keep you up nights and cripple you as long as you let it. Remember, *God did not give you the spirit of fear but one of power, love, and a sound mind* (2 Timothy 1:7).

Loneliness will tell you that you are all alone, and no one cares. It will try to isolate you and keep you away from others. It works through the father of lies, who will try to convince you that you have been rejected and abandoned. Remember, Jesus said *He would never leave you nor forsake you* (Hebrews 13:5).

Depression will do its best to bring you down to the lowest point and have you end it all. It thrives in misery and pain and doesn't want any form of joy or victory in your life. It tells you life is not worth living and will spin you around and around in its world of deception. Remember, *nothing is impossible with God and if God is for us, who can be against us?* (Luke 1:37; Romans 8:31).

Pride will rise up and say, "I'm perfectly capable of taking care of myself." It collaborates with human abilities to achieve impressive goals, until one morning you wake up and realize you have been detoured onto a dead-end road. Remember, *"God opposes the proud, but he gives grace to the humble"* (James 4:6).

These are just a few of the spiritual enemies that are at war with a believer, but these may be at the root of many different physical and/or mental conditions. Their main objective is to rob and steal from you and ultimately destroy you. The Word says that we wrestle against principalities, powers, and rulers of darkness, all of which are very real. As your passion for Christ increases, the greater the opposition will be. The good news is, you are not alone. Jesus is always there for you, tenderly watching and helping you. These battles are not meant as a hardship for you but a means of reshaping you. We need to have our self-centered pride "smashed," along with all the other human natural characteristics. More of you, less of me. Jesus overcame, and so can you. Surrender your will, believe His promises, and be obedient to His teachings. He said he would send a helper who would teach, remind, and guide you into all truth. Jesus told His disciples that in the world, they would have trouble and suffering, but they were to take courage.

Are you going to follow the road of human familiarity, or will you believe in Christ and walk committed to Him throughout life? I guarantee you there will be struggles and hardships if you say yes to the Lord, but our Lord promises to help you through each one. He will mold and form you into the person you were designed to be, so choose this day whom you will serve. If it's Christ, then don't expect easy, but someday, when you stand before God in a glorious white robe, you may hear, "Well done, good and faithful servant."

The Fight

The Lord is close to the brokenhearted and saves those
who are crushed in spirit.
—Psalm 34:18 (NIV)

How many times have you heard someone with health issues say, "I have a bad such-and-such"? God is good all the time, and what He created is good. At creation, He looked at man and said, "It is very good." At the fall, *bad* was introduced, and its purpose was to intentionally destroy the good God created.

So why is there disease, poverty, corruption, and so on? Because we live in a fallen world. During crisis times in life, we wrestle with God because the circumstances we are thrown into are not good and are potentially disastrous. Good was lost, and we are left with cruel and ugly. Our enemy is the author of disease, death, and destruction. We do not fight flesh and blood but rulers and principalities of the unseen world. We fight the thoughts of defeat and impossibilities, the notions that failure is all there is. We fight the lie that God isn't going to help us or the lie that He doesn't care. What God meant for good has been weakened but has not been destroyed. "O death, where is your victory? O death, where is your sting?" I love these verses in 2 Corinthians 4:8–9. "We are hard pressed on every side, but not crushed; perplexed, but not in despair; persecuted, but not abandoned; struck down, but not destroyed."

God has the final word. God is alive and comes close to the brokenhearted. It is hard to hold your life together when the bills need to be paid, and there isn't enough money to buy groceries. God is good all the time, and though you walk through the valley of the shadow of death, don't fear, for He is with you. He will strengthen you and carry you and will save all who are crushed in spirit. Agree with Him, and come against those powers that have come to rob, steal, and destroy. Take up the shield of faith, and trust the God who is alive and who is trustworthy.

Choose today to agree with God. Jesus did nothing apart from His father's will. He healed the sick, raised the dead, cast out demons, and restored people. Remember that Jesus loosed sickness, death, and demons from those He touched. He has the power. Nothing can destroy you—no sickness or demon. Your body may fade away but "the you inside" will live forever. *Selah.*

Hold on to Jesus. He has blown life into you, and someday He will take you home. Nothing in all of creation can change that.

The Road to Life

No man can serve two masters: for either he will hate the one, and love the other; or else he will hold to the one, and despise the other. You cannot serve God and mammon.
—Matthew 6:24 (KJV)

The road to life is certainly not easy. Those who are just beginning, think it will be smooth and pit-free, but they soon find robbers and thieves along the way. Huge forests are filled with snares, and old friends lure you back into the comfortable and familiar. The road to life is lonely, and you begin by putting one foot in front of the other, one day at a time.

There may be immediate successes as you travel forward, and those successes encourage you to go on. But what if there are no successes? Do not let the forest and the friends pull you back into the pit of despair or into the luring arms of desire. Remember where you were before your rescue. Were you frightened and in despair? Were you tormented? Were you stressed and unhappy? Was there any hope in your life? Remember where you were.

This road to life will lead you to a place of holiness, where you will finally be face-to-face with the one who has rescued you, the one who truly loves you and compassionately wants to give you hope and a future.

You hear the world telling you, "This is your last chance to have fun." This enemy is trying to deceive you and is telling lies. Going back is for fools, and doing so will only lead you back into bondage.

How do you know that the road ahead isn't filled with abundant joy? There could be freedom, there could be love, and there could be a purpose for your life. The answers are awaiting you. The question is, will you go? Will you go on this road in faith, believing and trusting in Jesus and His wonderful promises? Will it be an easy journey? I can guarantee you that it will not be easy, but I also guarantee you it will be worth it.

Fear and anxiety, along with self-pity—all self-centered threats—will most certainly confront you. When you're drowning with problems and unforeseen events, what do you do? Pull back, pray, and remember you have a God who says He will help you in your time of need. You have a Savior. The road to life is not easy. You must fight the enemies who are trying to stop you.

Which road will you follow—the road of the familiar and all the things you have known, or are you going to travel on the higher road? The higher road will bring life and get you to your destiny. It's your choice.

Choose whom you will serve this day—this world and its ruler, or God Almighty. Believing in what is seen and familiar will only get you more of what you already have. By believing in the unseen, you will experience far more than you could hope or imagine. Will it be easy? No. Nothing worth anything is easy.

Trials

We can rejoice, too, when we run into problems and trials,
for we know that they help us develop endurance.
—Romans 5:3 (NIV)

Trials are circumstances over which you have no control, and everyone has them at some time in his or her life. Actually, "trials have come so your faith may be proved genuine" (1 Peter 1:7). They are circumstances that affect you and those around you, either for good or bad. I have come to the conclusion that we move from one character-building trial to the next.

As hard as it is, we must stand and resist attacks that attempt to break us down and steal our joy. Will you give the enemy ground by believing his lies? Will you let self-pity take over, or will you believe the Word? Be a doer of the Word, not a hearer only. Stand in faith, and do not be overcome with doubt and fear.

When arrows fly from every direction, it is very difficult, humanly impossible, to stand. Fear, sadness, despair, hopelessness, pain, grief, and a host of other evil spirits and emotions will try to destroy you. At times I would cry out to God, "Where else can I go? Where else, Lord? I swallowed Christ, hook, line, and sinker, and there is no one else who can help me. If You, Lord, are not on my side, then who is? I must hold on. I must hold on. Help me, Lord, to hold on." In my anguish, Christ's words on the cross connected with my soul: "My God, my God, why have you forsaken me?" Jesus can identify with being alone in hours of great travail. Our cross will never be as heavy. You can endure. God is faithful.

When you pass through the waters, I will be with you;
and when you pass through the rivers, they will not sweep
over you. When you walk through the fire, you will not
be burned; the flames will not set you ablaze.
—Isaiah 43:1–3 (NIV)

Waiting is one of the most difficult lessons we need to learn. At times in my past, when I was overburdened with out-of-control circumstances flooding my life, I questioned God. I questioned His existence and even questioned if He cared. In the silent void, I wrestled with what I believed and why. Who was Jesus? As I pondered Jesus, I went back to what I knew to be true. I believe the Bible is true. I believe Jesus fulfilled every Messianic prophecy. I know there is historic documentation of His existence and Crucifixion in scripture. I looked at His answers when questioned, His compassion, and I even went back to my own life story and how I was changed that day so long ago. My conclusion? Jesus was the Messiah, God is real and alive, and what the Bible says about Him is true.

Questioning is good, as it solidifies what you believe. Sunday-school faith is like crawling; it works for a while but doesn't satisfy for long. Spiritual maturity is like walking or running. It takes muscles and balance, and muscles must be strengthened and developed. It all takes time.

Hardships develop spiritual muscles and cause us to press deep into God. It is difficult to go through valleys, to have every area of your life stripped away. I have had to learn to take every thought captive to the obedience of Christ and not let myself believe lies. Go back; look at your history. He was faithful to you in the past, and the Bible says He is the same yesterday, today, and tomorrow. Ponder Isaiah 43:1–3. God didn't say you weren't going to pass through the fire. He said, "you will not be burned; the flames will not set you ablaze." Don't trust your emotions, mind, or your heart; they are deceived.

In this hour, God is expecting maturity in His bride. We are to trust His Word alone and not lean on our own understanding. Go someplace special, sit, and just rest. Seek His presence. I often just sit in His presence, not expecting to hear or say anything. It has become my sanctuary of peace, my place of rest. Go to your special place, and let God tenderly hold you. Waiting is hard, but He will never leave you or forsake you.

What to Do with Reality

"When Jesus had finished saying all these things, he said to his
disciples, 'As you know, the Passover is two days away – and
the Son of Man will be handed over to be crucified …
While Jesus was in Bethany in the home of Simon the Leper, a woman
came to him with an alabaster jar of very expensive perfume, which
she poured on his head as he was reclining at the table. When the
disciples saw this, they were indignant. 'Why this waste?' they asked.
'This perfume could have been sold at a high price and the money
given to the poor.' Aware of this, Jesus said to them, 'Why are you
bothering this woman? She has done a beautiful thing to me. The poor
you will always have with you, but you will not always have me. When
she poured this perfume on my body, she did it to prepare me for
burial. Truly I tell you, wherever this gospel is preached throughout
the world, what she has done will also be told, in memory of her.'"
Matthew 26:1–2, 6–13 (NIV)

Jesus just announced that in a few days He would be "handed over to be crucified." What if my child were to tell me he only had days to live? I can't fathom my response! A woman, who may or may not have overheard Jesus, joined Jesus and the gathering at Simon's home and tenderly poured a very expensive perfume on Jesus. Each stroke of her hand on His head and feet tenderly massaged the oil into His skin. With real love, she followed her heart, doing the only thing she could. What wouldn't she give Him? She loves Him, and had she the sun, the moon, and the stars to give, even that would not be enough.

When my dad was dying, each touch of his hand was so endearing to me. I would sit for hours just petting his hand, knowing that at any time, he might be gone, and I would never have his hand to touch again. Love does strange things; raw emotions are vividly real.

Look in contrast to verses 8 and 9 in Matthew 26, which tell us the disciples' response to Jesus's prophetic declaration. Didn't they hear what Jesus had just told them minutes before? Did they not believe Him? Were they so distracted by this woman that they couldn't grasp what Jesus had just said? Were they so focused on what they thought to be a wasteful expenditure that they weren't able to understand the reality that was about to unfold? Were they insensitive, distracted, or nonbelieving?

Can you feel the emotion in these verses? Stop for a moment and try to put yourself into the story? Imagine if you had just heard Jesus say He was going to be crucified. *Selah.* What would you do with this reality? Would you enter into the pain and grief or disengage in unbelief? *Selah.*

When Life Is Hard

And we know that in all things God works for the good of those
who love him who have been called according to his purpose.
—Romans 8:28 (NASB)

God is sovereign, but He is not the orchestrator of disasters. On 9/11, the World Trade Center twin towers in New York came down, and thousands of people were hurt and killed. Was this in God's sovereign plan? Could God plan such a horrible disaster to bring us to our knees? That is not the God I know, so how do we explain such an event? When we are struck with real, painful life experiences we ask, "Where is He?" In Phillip Yancey's book *Disappointment with God*, Yancey tells the story of a woman who watched her twenty-year-old daughter die a painful death from cystic fibrosis. Both were believers. She said, "I will never forget those shrill, piercing, primal screams." Where was God, and why didn't He stop this from happening? Death/departure was not the enemy. To be absent from the body is to be present with the Lord, pain and disease were the enemies that attacked this young woman.

We all have times when we want to run and hide, far away from life's horrors. John the Baptist, in prison, sent his disciples to Jesus. Was he alerting Jesus of his imprisonment? Did John hope Jesus would come to rescue him? Jesus had said John was more than a prophet and was the greatest man born of woman, so it would have been a natural assumption that Jesus might help him. Why didn't Jesus help John? God didn't put John in prison; Herod did. Satan used Herod and Herodias to carry out his evil plan because Satan delights in destroying what is good.

This world is a war zone, with real battles going on between good and evil. Don't blame God for evil. He is good all the time and will never partake in darkness. Even though God is all-powerful, He will not force His will upon humankind. He, however, can work for the good of those who love Him. He is able to make a horror, like cystic fibrosis, end and can change mortality into immortality. He compassionately, tenderly, carries the grieving and provides grace upon grace to those who mourn. God's ways are so much higher than our ways. To try to understand why, is quite impossible, but we must trust Him. He will strengthen you and give you eyes to see. God is the author of all that is good.

Without a Vision

> Correct thy son, and he shall give thee rest; yea, he shall give delight unto thy soul. Where there is no vision, the people perish: but he that keepeth the law, happy is he.
> —Proverbs 29:17–18 (KJV)

The word *vision* means revelation, such as a prophet receives, and the words *the people perish* does not refer to unsaved people but a means to cast off restraint. The verse is stating that without God's Word, people cast off restraints to indulge the sinful nature. I once heard a speaker on *Focus on the Family* who told a story of two men. Both men were serious followers of Christ, reading their Bibles, studying the Word, praying, and holding each other accountable, but one day they posed a question: "What would happen if we were to stop everything for one week—no prayer, no time in the Word, no alone time, no accountability? What would happen?" They both agreed to the experiment. After one year, one of the men was able to get back on track, but his friend never returned. The speaker, who was the young man who had returned, gave his testimony of how difficult it was to return and lamented the loss of his friend.

Each society throughout history has had self-gratification attractively presented. Ultimately, it traps people into paganistic living. Without a clear understanding of God's plan, people—and not just the lost—cast off restraints to indulge their sinful natures, and just like the experiment of the two young men, some never return. The world's attraction can deceitfully lure believers away from God. When troubles and life circumstances weigh on the soul, a believer can be tempted to abandon the committed lifestyle and buy the lie.

Only understanding God's revelation for your life and exercising discipline will ultimately bring blessing and happiness. Don't fall prey to the snares of the fowler. It is like a bear trap that will not only cut off your leg but can kill you. Seek God's vision for your life. God has a vision for His people. Those who are called by His name are to turn from temporal gratification and trust Him for spiritual fulfillment and eternal joy. The revelation is God Himself, and it is only He who will bring you eternal peace and happiness. Seek Him while He can be found.

Chapter 10

TRUTH

How do you know what is true? Is there such a
thing as absolute truth? What do I know?
"Jesus told him, I am the way, the truth, and the life. No one
can come to the Father except through Me." John 14:6 (NLT)

Deception

The heart is deceitful above all things, and desperately wicked:
who can know it?
—Jeremiah 17:9 (KJV)

Deception is one of our worst enemies. Our sons and daughters go into the world and try to deal with life on their own. They face new jobs, friends, relationships, and basic daily tasks. How will they meet life's challenges? Who will they trust? They'll need to trust someone or something to survive.

The Bible says "our hearts are deceived," so we shouldn't trust ourselves to make godly decisions. In 2 Timothy 3, Paul describes the last days, and verse 13 says there will be those who deceive and people who will be deceived. In Matthew 24, Jesus says to watch out that no one deceives you.

Try as we might, decisions are made with only partially available information, but what about the facts we don't know? It's easy to know the right thing to do after something has happened but very difficult to know what to do beforehand. Where is God in all this? Are we seeking God's Word for direction, or are we calling on our own understanding?

Since the fall, people's decision making comes from within their own reasoning. The enemy tells us to think for ourselves, and we don't need to consult God. Pride that has come from humankind's rebellion says we are capable and able of doing whatever we want to do, and we don't need God to tell us what to do. Satan beckons us to be rebellious toward God, and our rebellious, deceptive hearts are exposed when our desire to live without God's intervention becomes our normal.

God has established helpful indicators to help you draw on the truth and not be deceived. When you wrestle with what to do, exercise your right as a child of God and ask Him. When that strange *peace* comes over you, follow it. That peace is an indicator of a right choice. *Agreement* is another indicator. If two or more trustworthy friends or family sense the same thing, follow it.

As I pray, God will often tell me to go to an authority figure, such as a spouse, pastor, or godly person to *seek counsel*. The Lord has always sent me to the right person, and that person has always been used by God to point me in the right direction.

Always pray. The Lord will guide you in whatever you do. Don't rush the decision-making process. The devil wants to push you into a hasty decision, but Jesus will always gently lead you. Wait to hear; wait for that peace and be still. The Lord is faithful and will answer and direct you in the way you should go. He is the Creator, the Alpha and the Omega, and He knows all things, including the seen and unseen. He alone knows the best for your life. You just need to ask, so talk to God.

Let the Heavens

The heavens declare the glory of God; the skies proclaim the work of his hands. Day after day they pour forth speech; night after night they display knowledge. There is no speech or language where their voice is not heard. Their voice goes out into all the earth, their words to the ends of the world. In the heavens he has pitched a tent for the sun.
—Psalm 19:1–4 (NIV)

For since the creation of the world His invisible attributes, His eternal power and divine nature, have been clearly seen, being understood through what has been made, so that they are without excuse.
—Romans 1:20 (NASB)

Is there any part of creation that does not testify of God? Whatever we see and whatever our senses tell us, we tend to believe. Our minds are not likely to gravitate toward the unseen, so typically our subconscious controls how we look at things. Take, for instance, winter in South Dakota. Automatically, we think of cold and can't wait until it warms up. However, look deeper at winter, and don't focus on the negative but on the positive. Let's look at how God's invisible attributes are seen in winter.

I love the snow and how it covers all the ugly, dormant ground beneath. I love to look at the geese swimming in the open water. I love to snuggle up in front of a warm fireplace. I love wearing beautiful sweaters that keep me warm. Where do I see God in these things? The snow-covered ground reminds me of the blood of Christ that covers me, making me as white as snow. The geese remind me of the protection of God that is all around me, and when I am in open, frigid water, His protection is my covering. I see God in the warmth of a fireplace because great grace permits me to sit quietly in restful peace at the feet of Jesus. And finally, my warm sweaters remind me of those my mother used to make me. She made me those sweaters to demonstrate her love for me. God loves me and He has made all things new. His love is never too big or small; it is always just right. It wraps around me and keeps me warm.

Perspective is how you look at things. Let the creation around you proclaim the work of His hands. There are so many clues that show God's master design. How wonderful that He wants to reveal Himself. It is difficult not to experience God when the sun rises and the colors of a new morning cut through the night sky, or when you bite into a fresh peach on a warm summer day, or you hear your son play a piano scherzo by Chopin, or you smell chocolate cookies in the oven. God saw what He had created was good. Look for God today. His evidences are all around you.

No Condemnation

"For those who live according to the flesh set their minds on the things of the flesh, but those who live according to the Spirit, (set their minds on) the things of the Spirit"
—Romans 8:5 (ESV)

There is no condemnation for those who are in Christ Jesus. No past sin or past deed can condemn we who are in Christ. Jesus died that we may have life. Jesus came to undo what Adam did. Adam's spirit died when he disobeyed God's command not to eat of the fruit, but Jesus did not follow His fleshly desires. He did nothing apart from the Father's will. Even in the garden, in agony, he prayed that the cup be removed. "Yet, not my will but thine be done." Jesus took upon Himself every charge Satan uses against us and through His forgiveness, every sin, every mistake, every failure is truly washed away. So if you are hearing condemnation, it is not coming from God.

When you are born again, the Spirit of *life* comes into you, making you fully alive with Christ, canceling *everything* against you (Colossians 2:13–14) and *permanently* sealing you (Ephesians 1:13). You were dead in your trespass and sin, but through Christ, God has made you alive.

At one point in every human life, we all have walked fully in the flesh, giving the flesh exactly whatever it demanded. When our eyes were opened to the work of Jesus, the Holy Spirit came into us, linking us to God, back to a pre-fall position. When Christ Jesus sets us free from the law of sin and death, we are free to love, free to have joy and peace, free to be patient and kind toward others, and actually free to be good and faithful.

Freedom in Christ goes against every learned behavior up to the point of your salvation. You don't have to do what you have done in the past. You are free to live differently. Call upon the Spirit to help you, and remember that Jesus came so that you may have life, not death. He overcame, and so can you. His Spirit did not die on that cross, but His flesh, mind, will, and emotions all died. His Spirit could not die. His Spirit is what raised Him from the dead. His Spirit is the same Spirit that lives in us. Hallelujah! Rejoice and be glad. You were once dead, but now you are alive; once blind but now can see.

Prayer:

Lord, let the Holy Spirit of God have His way in my life. Fix my mind on the things above. Help me to love, not hate; give, not take; have pure thoughts, not negative, judgmental thoughts. Let me be able to forgive and not be vindictive. God, help me to have the mind of Christ and to love others as You love me.

Yet to all who received him, to those who believed in his
name, he gave the right to become children of God.
—John 1:12 (NIV)

The existence of something is reality, and whether or not we know of it or believe in it does not change the fact. The cell is the smallest living thing; humans are composed of roughly ten trillion cells divided into about two hundred different types. Our muscles are made of muscle cells; our livers, liver cells; skin, skin cells—cells for everything in the body. There are even specialized types of cells that make the enamel for our teeth and the clear lenses in our eyes. Long before you and I were aware of cells, they existed. I don't know much about them and certainly can't fathom the complexities of how they work, but whether I understand or not, believe it or not, accept it or not, they exist.

The same is true about heaven and hell. Heaven and hell are real places, and just because someone doesn't believe they exist doesn't negate the reality of their existence. The word *heaven* is mentioned in both the Old and New Testaments 582 times in the King James Version of the Bible, and hell or Hades is mentioned fifty-four times in the King James Bible. However, Jesus spoke of hell more than heaven.

Of the 1,850 verses in the New Testament that record
Jesus' words, 13 percent of them deal with the subject
of eternal judgment and hell. In fact, Jesus spoke more
frequently about hell than He did about heaven.
—Robert Jeffress, *How Can I Know?*

A few years ago, I read the book *90 Minutes in Heaven*. The author was in a serious car accident and was pronounced legally dead. For ninety minutes he was absent from this world but fully alive in heaven. His description of who and what he saw is truly amazing. My father's nurse, who previously had worked on the oncology floor of the hospital, had many experiences with dying patients. I asked her if there was any truth to the stories I had heard about people seeing angels, for example, moments before death. She said, "Oh yes, some patients would see family members or children they had lost in the room, while others vividly saw angels." They could see things she couldn't.

Two real places: heaven and hell. Heaven—a place where God will dwell with His created beings forever, a beautiful place, free from bondage, disease, pain, and evil of all kinds, where love abounds, and life will be as originally designed.

Hell was never meant for human beings but was a place designed for Satan and the fallen angels to receive their eternal punishment. It is a place of torment, anguish, horror, and regret, where fire and thirst cannot be quenched.

God wills that none shall perish but all have eternal life. We all must choose either to be with our Creator or separated from Him. Why would anyone choose not to accept this free gift of salvation? Why wouldn't anyone accept purity over evil, love over hate, life over punishment, or joy over grief? I don't have all the understanding or all the answers to the mysteries of God, but I can and have accepted them in faith. Jesus offers heaven to each of us; it is His gift to us. Have you received it?

Submit and Follow

How many times have you heard Christians say, "Well, I believe …" or "Well, I think …"? Is it up to us to know all the facts and come to a conclusion? Or, is it our job to read the Word, talk to God, and to follow His advice, when questions arise? How can we fully know about something that we know nothing about? One of my favorite expressions is, "you don't know what you don't know." We don't know everything but God does. Go to His Word and base your decision on His truths. We are human, but He is *God*. He will direct us if we genuinely seek the truth. He has given us a love letter to instruct us. The Bible seems contrary to how this world has taught us to behave. It totally messes with our worldviews, but if we disregard our human responses and follow His directives, we will experience a positively profound result. We do not understand His ways, but we are given the ability through His Spirit to trust Him, and the ability to agree and follow, no matter what.

The battle is in our minds. Do we believe what God says, or do we believe what we want to believe? Which one? To follow God is not easy. Living life is hard enough on its own, but when difficulties with children, parents, spouses, jobs, finances, are added on top of an already stretched life, it is next to impossible to make healthy decisions. How on earth can we expect to have all the answers when our lives' are stressed and we don't have all the facts? Pause, seek God's help, ask for His advise, and don't just react.

I know that God wins this great war. All who believe and put their trust in him will not perish. You will suffer many hardships, so do not let discouragement into your heart. Rise up in faith and trust our Lord. Take the *time* to seek His help. You will overcome.

Such a Great Salvation

How shall we escape if we ignore such a great salvation?
This salvation, which was first announced by the Lord,
was confirmed to us by those who heard him.
—Hebrews 2:3 (NIV)

This morning as I was sitting beside my warm fireplace on this very cold day, I was thinking of our Father God's having to watch His Son's death. I can't imagine watching your child die a torturous death of any kind, more so on a cross. A song kept running through my mind: "When I survey that wondrous cross on which the Prince of Glory died, all the vain things that charmed me the most, I sacrifice them to His blood." What love the

Father has for us. There is very little chance that I would sacrifice my son for anyone, but God sent His Son to die for all of us who had abandoned, despised, and rejected Him.

The Roman soldiers had twisted together a crown of thorns and shoved it into His head; a purple robe was placed on his raw back. He was mocked, laughed at, despised, and rejected by men, and we esteemed him not. He was nailed to a cross while the Father and the host of heaven watched, not one went to save Him. I wonder if they were tempted to help their Jesus.

The world is filled with millions who don't believe there is a need to forgive sin because they don't believe in sin. Relativism erases conviction, and humanism satisfies self-centeredness and replaces the need for a Savior.

Does that mean if they don't believe in God or the importance of salvation that it isn't true? Some argue the existence of God is real, while others say it is fiction. It is either all true or all false, but just because people do not accept Christ doesn't mean Christ wasn't God incarnate. Just because some do not call sin as sin doesn't mean there is not an absolute right or wrong. If people don't believe in Jesus, and their intellect has made them rulers of their own lives, then how can we approach them with the message of such a great salvation? For the agnostic and atheist, convincing arguments, in my opinion, will make no difference. Like us at the moment when our eyes were unveiled, they too need the Holy Spirit to unveil their eyes to see Jesus and to grasp the enormity of His love.

Love, prayer, and the Word of God will avail much. The combination of these three put into action is a powerful force. Love them, pray for them, and speak the Word of God over them in prayer, and watch God be God. He will accomplish and achieve His purpose for His glory.

The Trinity

Praise be to the God and Father of our Lord Jesus Christ! In
his great mercy he has given us new birth into a living hope
through the resurrection of Jesus Christ from the dead.
—1 Peter 1:3 (NIV)

But when the Helper comes, whom I shall send to you from the Father,
the Spirit of truth who proceeds from the Father, He will testify of Me.
—John 15: 26 (NIV)

For there are three that bear witness in heaven: The Father,
the Word, and the Holy Spirit; and these three are one.
—1 John 5:7 (NIV)

Peter praises the God and Father of our Lord Jesus, the four gospels reveal Jesus, and Jesus tells his disciples of a comforter—three very distinct persons. In 1 John 5:7, the word *one* means unity. The three are one in unity, yet three in individuality—one God the Father, one Lord Jesus Christ, and one Holy Spirit. Individually, each is called God, and collectively they are called God.

The Father is the head of Christ, the Son is the redeemer of humankind, and the Holy Spirit is the helper. Too many of us conglomerate the three Godheads into one, without giving much thought to their individual personalities, but it's wise to meditate upon each and the characteristic they represent.

Water, for example, illustrates an element with distinctly different functions—solid, liquid, or mist. All are water but with different appearances and different functions. In much the same way, we have a Father who is always available at any time to hear our concerns and whose *genuine* unconditional love and wisdom we never need to doubt. We have a mother figure in Jesus, who actually gave Himself for those he loves. He was and is and will ever be compassionately merciful toward His own. And we have the Holy Spirit, who continually points us to our role model, Jesus, and whose steadfast friendship stands ready with a listening ear to help us.

The Father, the Son, and Holy Spirit—three very distinct persons with three distinctly different job descriptions, yet one in perfect unity. When you talk to God, to which one of the three are you talking? Which one do you go to with your troubles to receive wisdom? Which one will nurture and tenderly care for you? Which one will you call upon as you walk through life? Meditate on the three, and let the Holy Spirit teach you about the Father, the Son, and Himself.

What Do You Know?

"What do you know?" is a very easy question to ask but a very difficult question to answer. We think we know, but do we? Peter said to Jesus, "even if I have to die with You, I will not deny you" (Matthew 26:35). Peter thought he would never deny Jesus. History tells us differently. Peter thought he was doing the right thing when he cut off the ear of the man arresting Jesus. He assumed, acting out of his human nature, that he was protecting Jesus. He didn't know the complexity of God's plan of salvation. I catch myself saying, "I know." Once the Lord said to me, "What do you know?" It was then that I first realized how much I assume I know when, in fact, I do not know all the facts because I have such a limited vantage point.

As we stumble through this life, are we making the right decisions? Humans are finite, seeing only in part. Each day we are confronted with decision making, drawn from our limited insights and perspectives. Insignificant calls really don't change our lives (like whether to choose coffee or tea), but what about whom to marry or deciding a career path? That decision may put you on a path headed toward or away from your destiny, or is there a specific destined path? Will God show us exactly where we are to be, or will He only help us in whatever way we choose? *Selah*. Remember we have been created with free will. We have a choice; we haven't been robotically programmed.

Trusting God, who knows all things, and leaning on His Holy Spirit is the only way we can move effectively through life. With whatever door opens before you, ask the question, "Could this be where God wants me?" If we are honest with ourselves, we can't know anything for certain. We may think we know our feelings until circumstances change. We may think we know the direction we are going until there is a divorce, a death, or another job opportunity. So how do we know? We pray. Scripture tells us not to lean on our own understanding but to trust God in all things, and He will make our paths straight. Learn to wait until you hear that still small voice and receive peace from God.

So what do we actually know? I know that Christ lived and died, and like Paul, I know Christ was crucified. All of the other daily circumstances I encounter can change. Life is uncertain, but God wants to walk with us day by day. He remains the same. Ask for His help and guidance, and then trust Him.

Make a list of things that you actually know, and then ask God if the list is accurate.

What Is in a Word?

The Son is the radiance of God's glory and the exact representation of his being, sustaining all things by his powerful word. After he had provided purification for sins, he sat down at the right hand of the Majesty in heaven.
—Hebrews 1:3 (NIV)

Being confident of this, that he who began a good work in you will carry it on to completion until the day of Christ Jesus.
—Philippians 1:6 (NIV)

What is in a word? Look at the word *sat*. Jesus sat down at the right hand of God. The priests in the temple never sat down. The temple had the brass altar, the laver, the table of showbread, the altar of incense, the golden candlestick, and the ark of the covenant. There were no chairs; a priest's work was ongoing. Year after year, they continually offered sacrifices for the sins of the people. Their work was never complete. However, Jesus sat down because He had completed His work, once and for all—past, present, future. So being confident with what He began in you, *He will carry it to completion*. Wow! He is sitting beside the Father, not worried, not fretful, but completely confident that His sacrifice was and is sufficient for you and me, saving forever those who draw near (Hebrews 7:25).

I often think of one word and ask the Holy Spirit to teach me. Once, I meditated upon the word *in*. What did it mean to be "in Christ"? To be in something meant to be within, surrounded by, included within. Reflecting only on this alone, I could see how deep the scriptures are, as well as the very depth of God's love for me. If anything tries to capture me, it must go through Christ first to get to me. If I am *in* Christ, can I ever separate myself from Christ? The Word says nothing can separate me from His love, but could I separate myself from Him and go my own way. Would that somehow undermine the sufficiency of the cross? *Selah*. I believe I can walk away from Him physically, but why would I? *Selah*. There wouldn't be protection, and I would have to fend for myself. Why would I ever go back into captivity? Think about it. Isn't it better to trust God than to go it alone without help? I don't know everything, but God does, so why would I think I could live without His guidance? The devil would like to temp me to believe I would be happier or more successful, but I've been down that road and don't ever want to believe that pack of lies again. Alone, separated from God—how horrible? I can't imagine!

There is so much depth in meditating upon a word. Explore the endless depth of the Word as the Holy Spirit draws you deeper. Christ promises us that He will carry us through. His work is finished. Rest in His faithfulness.

> Stretch out your hand to heal and perform miraculous signs
> and wonders through the name of your holy servant Jesus.
> —Acts 4:30 (NIV)

Miracles, signs, and wonders impact greatly those who do not know the Lord. They are a profound testimony, a supernatural declaration of the existence of a real God who is able to break natural barriers.

At times in the past, the Gallup poll has attempted to define evangelicals as those who answer affirmatively to three questions:

1. Have you been born again, or have you had a born-again experience?
2. Have you encouraged other people to believe in Jesus Christ?
3. Do you believe the Bible is the actual word of God?

In 1980, about 19 percent of the adult population agreed with all three statements. In a Gallup poll update in May 2007, 22 percent of all Americans agreed with all three statements. Even more elaborate criteria have been used by other researchers. One research firm, the Barna Group, argues that individuals must answer positively to as many as nine different questions in order to qualify as evangelical. Not surprisingly, only 7 percent of the US adult population qualifies as evangelical using these restrictive criteria.

A segment in the documentary *Supersize Me* showed the effectiveness of advertising. Children were shown a series of pictures and asked to identify the people pictured. A few kids recognized the first picture—a portrait of George Washington. No one recognized the individual in the next picture. The picture was turned toward the camera, and to my disbelief, it was a picture of Jesus. Not one of the children could identify Jesus. If I had not seen it, I would not have believed it. The kids were shown another picture, and this time all of the children knew the face—it was Ronald McDonald.

Americans have gone throughout the world as missionaries, yet in our own nation, there is a huge population who have never heard of and can't identify Christ. Who will go to America? But how will they know unless we tell them? God's miracles, signs, and wonders open blind eyes to the reality of God. Although God is perfectly capable of doing all the work, He has chosen to work through us. We are to go into the world with the gospel. Look around you. This nation needs you.

Chapter 11

SPIRITUAL GROWTH FREEDOM

*I pray you will be given "a spirit of wisdom and of
revelation in the knowledge of Him..." and "the eyes of
your heart may be enlightened so that you will know the
hope of His calling..." Ephsians 1:17, 18 (NAS)*

And their houses shall be turned unto others, with their fields and wives together: for I will stretch out my hand upon the inhabitants of the land, saith the LORD. For from the least of them even unto the greatest of them every one is given to covetousness; and from the prophet even unto the priest every one dealeth falsely. They have healed also the hurt of the daughter of my people slightly, saying, Peace, peace; when there is no peace. Were they ashamed when they had committed abomination? Nay, they were not at all ashamed, neither could they blush: therefore they shall fall among them that fall: at the time that I visit them they shall be cast down, saith the LORD. Thus saith the LORD, *Stand ye in the ways, and see, and ask for the old paths, where is the good way,* and walk therein, and ye shall find rest for your souls. But they said, We will not walk therein. Also I set watchmen over you, saying, Hearken to the sound of the trumpet. But they said, We will not hearken.
—Jeremiah 6:12–18 (KJV, emphasis added)

We have all fallen short of the glory of God, and all, like sheep, have gone astray. No matter if others say, "That's all right," sin is sin no matter if one believes it or not. In this passage, God's people aren't ashamed of their behavior and don't know how to blush. What they are watching and doing doesn't embarrass them anymore because they have grown tolerant of evil. Sound familiar? No matter what the world thinks, there is a holy God who says, "There is a right road. Walk on it."

The flesh wants to do what the flesh wants to do, and the mind, most of the time, is in full agreement with the flesh. The Spirit of God says, "No, stop; it's wrong," but that still small voice is being ignored. God has sent godly leaders to proclaim truth. Are we listening? Are we turning off our TVs or switching the channel? Some spiritual shepherds, as we have learned, are preaching out of their woundedness, rather than adhering to the Word of God.

In Jeremiah 6:16, God says, we are to stand and ask for the ancient paths—former ways. We are not to go on; we are to go back. Go back to the ancient paths. Go back to the Word of God. Remember when Isaac, in Genesis 26, was looking for water for his flocks. He went back and reopened the wells his father had dug. There, he found fresh water for his sheep.

In a day when so much error is coming at us, stop, turn back to God's Word, and listen to God's voice. Do not let the flesh dictate what you should or should not do. Trust in God alone, always listen, and respond to His still small voice. Relativism has brainwashed much of America and has put her off course. The only way for her to move forward is by turning back to her roots and become a nation under God.

Balance

> The LORD abhors dishonest scales, but accurate weights are
> his delight. When pride comes, then comes disgrace, but with
> humility comes wisdom. The integrity of the upright guides
> them, but the unfaithful are destroyed by their duplicity.
> —Proverbs 11:1–3 (NET)

It would be very hard to walk down a flight of stairs if you had no sense of equilibrium. Life depends on balance, and when life's balances are disturbed, noticeable consequences result. There is balance in nature, balance in eating, balance in nutrition, pressure balances, and balance in relationships. God first created man for Himself. Then He created a partner for man, then children, and finally He instructed them to take care of the garden and all that He had created. When God's order is sustained, restful balance is maintained.

God never tugs and never gives you more than you can bear. His yoke is easy, and His burden light. He gently leads. Satan, on the other hand, tugs hard and pushes until there is no time to sit at the feet of Jesus, no time to spend with your spouse, no time to love on your kids. We find ourselves falling down the stairs because life's extremes have thrown our equilibrium off-kilter. Carrots are nutritious, but if we ate only carrots, our skin would turn orange. Well, if you are turning orange, stop eating so many carrots. All extremes are harmful and will disturb stability.

As believers, how do we maintain equilibrium? Look to Jesus, who humbly served, gently guided, and taught those He loved. He didn't hurry through anything or give his followers more than they could handle. He maintained balance. God sees everything you are experiencing. Are you trusting Him to answers your questions? Are you praying for His solutions for your needs? Are you maintaining His peace in your daily life?

God's Word is true and trustworthy. Life is fragile, and equilibrium can be lost if it's not protected. He has said He will care for you and supply every need. Trust Him. He has a plan for your life. Get your priorities in order; they always will maintain balance.

Eagles

Like an eagle that stirs up its nest and hovers over its young, that spreads its wings to catch them and carries them on its pinions.
—Deuteronomy 32:11 (NIV)

One of the most picturesque examples of God's wonderful, protective guiding hand is found in Deuteronomy 32:11. When the baby eaglets are ready to fledge, the mother eagle actually pushes her little ones, one by one, out of her nest. As the eaglet plummets from the cliff above toward the rocks below, the mother swoops beneath her little one, catching it on her large, majestic wings. The process continues until the eaglet learns to flap its wings, and once the baby has experienced this, it will no longer need to be pushed out. It will spread its grand wings on its own and soar.

We can listen to the best instructors and learn the complexities of any given subject, but until we experience it, we cannot come close to a real understanding. Experience is the best teacher. If the mother eagle never pushed her young out of their towering nest, the baby would never learn how to fly. He could watch flying endlessly, but until he experiences flight, he will not understand how being pushed out of the nest could be for his good. It takes falling. Basic instinct kicks in only after he is pushed out.

My son Joseph came home after college and settled into our home. Weeks passed without any thought of moving. One day, I had a little talk with Joe. I wasn't helping him by allowing him to live there. I told him I would help him find an apartment and would pray for him to find a job. It was hard for me to see him go out on his own, but I knew the time had come for him to lean on God, not me. He made mistakes along the way, but by pushing him out of the nest, he had to learn that God was real and faithful. He developed spiritual muscles and learned how to fly. Today, he and his three brothers have all become amazing men of God.

Leaders should neither smother their spiritual young nor keep them in their nest. They should release them to become who God intended them to be. The mother bird knows the time to release those who are ready, as should spiritual leaders. Upon their release, they will catch the wind and soar.

Resist the temptation to stay well fed in that comfortable, warm nest. When the time is right, your spiritual guardian needs to push you out so you can soar on wings like eagles. God intended you to fly.

Emergency Numbers—More Effective than 911

Use these emergency numbers in the following situations:

When you are sad, phone John 14.
When you have sinned, phone Psalm 51.
When you are facing danger, phone Psalm 91.
When people have failed you, phone Psalm 27.

When it feels as though God is far from you, phone Psalm 139.

When your faith needs stimulation, call Hebrews 11.

When you are alone and scared, phone Psalm 23.

When you are worried, phone Matthew 8:19–34.

When you are hurt and criticized, call 1 Corinthians 13.

When you wonder about Christianity, phone 2 Corinthians 5:15–18.

When you feel like an outcast, phone Romans 8:31–39.

When you are seeking peace, phone Matthew 11:25–30.

When it feels as if the world is bigger than God, phone Psalm 90.

When you need Christ like insurance, phone Romans 8:1–30.

When you are leaving home for a trip, phone Psalm 121.

When you are praying for yourself, phone Psalm 87.

When you require courage for a task, phone Joshua 1.

When inflation and investments are hogging your thoughts, phone Mark 10:17–31.

When you are depressed, phone Psalm 27.

When your bank account is empty, phone Psalm 37.

When you lose faith in humankind, phone 1 Corinthians 13.

When it looks like people are unfriendly, phone John 15.

When you are losing hope, phone Psalm 126.

When you feel the world is small compared to you, call Psalm 19.

When you want fruit, phone John 15.

When you want Paul's secret for happiness, phone Colossians 3:12–17.

When you have a big opportunity or discovery, phone Isaiah 55.

When you want to get along with others, phone Romans 12.

Alternate Numbers

For dealing with fear, call Psalm 47.

For security, call Psalm 121:3.

For assurance, call Mark 8:35.

For reassurance, call Psalm 145:18.

All these numbers may be phoned directly.

All lines to heaven are available twenty-four hours a day.

Feed your faith, and doubt will starve to death.

—author unknown

Mary Swift Kelly

God's Economy

> Now to him who is able to do immeasurably more than all we ask
> or imagine, according to his power that is at work within us.
> —Ephesians 3:20 (NIV)

Can an acorn tell you what it is like to be an oak tree? Can a child plunking away on a piano tell you what it is like to play Carnegie Hall? Imagination can take you only so far, but how do you know what you do not know? As I age, I'm amazed at all the new innovations and technologies that make life easier. I once used a typewriter, paper, eraser, envelope, and a stamp to send a message, but now I use a wireless laptop computer with a 10.5 operating system, instant data correction, spell-check, and e-mail that instantly transfers messages to multiple receivers.

Humans are upgraded continually with new information; we need to be learning constantly. The kingdom of God operates in the same manner. We see a need, we ask in prayer, and the Spirit answers. We follow God's response, and God's will is done. God continually gives us His solutions, which far surpass our wildest imaginations or natural thinking, and the more we see God responding, the more we desire His ways. He is brilliant. Why wouldn't we want His solutions?

God loves giving. The more you freely give, the more He freely gives back to you. God loves serving. The more you freely serve, the more He blesses you. The same is true with righteousness. The more you bow, submitting to God's ways, the more righteous you become. He nudges, you're obedient, and then He delights in blessing. Think of the other virtues where this applies. It is His economy, the process of learning. God is teaching.

Just as a walnut tree produces walnuts, we will bear only that which is in us. Luke 6 says righteousness is a matter of the heart. If the motive behind the desire is wrong, check your heart, but if the motive comes from a loving obedient heart, then blessings will flow.

The enemy would like to make us believe that if we give, we will not have enough, or if we submit to God's ways, we are weaklings. I say that God has a bigger plan for you, something greater than you know. Continue to walk toward Him, and He will direct your path. Continue to seek His ways, and He will provide and protect you from the fowler's snares. He is able to do immeasurably more than you could hope or imagine.

The acorn can become a majestic oak tree, and a child playing "Chopsticks" can perform at Carnegie Hall. It takes good soil and lots of practice.

Jesus Came

For even the Son of Man did not come to be
served, but to serve, and to give his life
as a ransom for many.
—Mark 10:45 (NIV)

One of the reasons Jesus came was because of His love to serve. He came for the sick and the lost. He was a radical lover; compassionate about those He had created. Then He ascended, leaving the charge for His disciples to do what He had done. Whenever we choose to isolate ourselves, either alone or with other believers, there should be a check in your spirit. We have been called to be laborers in the harvest fields. Our Christian walk should not be self-motivated, it should constantly resemble Jesus, who did not do His own will but the Father's will. We are to humble ourselves and submit lovingly to serve others, always keeping our eyes fixed upon Jesus and following His example. We can learn so much from those we have selectively overlooked. The Holy Spirit will open our eyes to the real need of others, if we are willing.

God requires more from us than the giving of material goods. As someone once said, "Put feet to your words." It is a privilege and a joy to serve the people God places around us. It's a reward that far outweighs the time and effort invested. I believe it is a kingdom principle that commands a blessing.

Prayer:

Holy Spirit, check our spirits and show us ways we can serve those we live and work around. Do not let us turn a deaf ear to their voices that cry out in need. Help us to lovingly give time and words of life, wonderful treasures that will not come back void but actually will achieve God's purpose.

Liberty to the Captive

The Spirit of the Lord GOD is upon me; because the LORD
hath anointed me to preach good tidings unto the meek; he hath
sent me to bind up the brokenhearted, to proclaim liberty to the
captives, and the opening of the prison to them that are bound.
—Isaiah 61:1 (KJ)

The Spirit of the Lord is upon me, because he hath anointed me
to preach the gospel to the poor; he hath sent me to heal the
brokenhearted, to preach deliverance to the captives, and recovering
of sight to the blind, to set at liberty them that are *bruised*.
—Luke 4:18 (KJ)

God did not give laws commanding slavery, nor did He advocate the oppression of people. Bondage is a human invention. Our fallen condition enslaves, oppresses, and keeps others captive, preventing them from exercising their free will. Jesus came to set the brokenhearted, distressed, troubled, blind, and *captive* free from their enslaved condition. This liberty was to be proclaimed.

Today there is little thought of slavery, yet people are enslaved all around us—some physically, some emotionally, some spiritually. Christ used the word *bruised*, referring to those who are completely crushed and whose lives have been shattered, those oppressed and broken in body and soul, and those who have no desire to live. This oppression is slavery, no matter what you may think.

Jesus came to set people free. You may ask, "Where do I see slavery?" I see it in an abused wife or child who, out of fear, cannot get away; in a teenager who wants to commit suicide; in an alcoholic; a drug or gambling addict; a man who cheats on his wife, physically or through pornography; in a wife's silence, ignoring her husband; or in a person who actually is a slave of another for profit.

Jesus came to set them free. The freedom Jesus speaks about is still available. Satan works through the mind, and if his message that "nothing can change and there is no hope" is believed, the enslavement hook is set. You are as bound as you think you are. Invite Christ to open the prison doors of your mind, and let Him deliver you, heal you, and set you free.

My Chains Are Off

You used to walk in these ways, in the life you once lived.
—Colossians 3:7 (NIV)

For God has not given us a spirit of fear and timidity,
but of power, love, and self-discipline.
—2 Timothy 1:7 (NLT)

Once when visiting a prison in Argentina, I saw an assembly of inmates praising God with such genuine worship that they were totally unaware that our group of fifteen had entered the room. These men, who were behind bars physically, were absolutely free, spiritually. Scripture says, "You used to walk in these ways, in the life you once lived"; a life that keeps you enslaved by anger, rage, malice, slander, fear, gossip, cruelty, manipulation, sexual immorality, impurity, lust, and greed, to name a few. Worldly prisons keep people captive and under the prison's control. As humans, we often are blind and unaware that something is controlling us.

Lyrics from a Chris Tomlin song tell us:

My chains are gone
I have been set free
My God, my Savior has ransomed me
And like a flood His mercy reigns
Unending love, amazing grace

What do these lyrics mean? The choice is ours; freedom is available. Chains can come off. Fear manipulates people to live within prisons in their own minds, but the Word says "we have not been given a spirit of fear," so identify the things that hold you captive. Jesus said He came to set captives free. God works with us to open prison doors, but the desire to rid these demons from our lives must be real. Freedom is the light at the end of that dark tunnel.

Great Britain abolished the slave trade two hundred years ago. As slaves, these people were removed from their homes and families and imprisoned, forced to adapt to captivity. It is difficult to think that we are slaves being held captive, but in fact, we are slaves held captive to controlling habits or addictions. We were born blind into this world, and only freedom in Christ can bring sight. Ask the Lord to open your eyes to the things that are holding you. Big things are easy to see, but what about hidden things, like fear? Fear of talking, fear of raising your hands in worship, fear of witnessing—you can be totally unaware of what is holding you. Ask the Lord to reveal the things in your life that are keeping you from being free, and then, little by little, follow His escape plan. The Colossians verse says "once were"; it implies believers have escaped and have broken free. We all have the ability to escape. We simply need to identify the strongholds in our lives and, with the guidance of the Holy Spirit, move with God toward freedom.

Therefore, prepare your minds for action; be self-controlled; set your hope fully on the grace to be given you when Jesus Christ is revealed. As obedient children, do not conform to the evil desires you had when you lived in ignorance. But just as he who called you is holy, so be holy in all you do; for it is written: "Be holy, because I am holy." (1 Peter 1:13–16)

As those who have experienced the "new birth" (1 Peter 1:3), Christians are expected to live on a higher moral plane than the ungodly citizens of the world. The lifestyle expected of us is called "holy living." (Taken from *The Expository Files*, a monthly electronic journal, edited by Warren E. Berkley and Jon W. Quinn)

New Wineskins

> To make her holy, cleansing her by the washing
> with water through the word.
> —Ephesians 5:26 (NIV)

> And no one pours new wine into old wineskins. If he does, the new wine
> will burst the skins, the wine will run out and the wineskins will be
> ruined. No, new wine must be poured into new wineskins. And no one
> after drinking old wine wants the new, for he says, 'The old is better.'
> —Luke 5:37–39 (NIV)

When referring to wine, the word *new* means fresh or young, but when referring to wineskins, it means renewal.

A wineskin was made from an entire tanned goatskin, with the legs and tails removed and sealed. The new wine was poured into the large skin, and during the fermentation process, carbon dioxide gas would stretch the skin to its limit. Once the wineskin was used, it would lose its ability to stretch again, *unless* it was soaked in water. Those who could not afford new skins would soak the old skin in water to regain its elasticity.

How do we stay flexible in whatever the Lord might do in our lives? Make it a priority to bath yourself in the Word and digest what the Spirit of God is saying. It will have a renewing effect. Past emersion in the Word is good, but the daily reading of the Word will regenerate new revelations and understandings. One of the ways God speaks to us is through the Word, and everyday life brings with it new challenges with different circumstances that need new answers.

God says to "wash with water through the Word" and let the Holy Spirit help lead you daily.

God's love is for humankind—for all who are hungry, sorrowful, oppressed, scorned, mistreated, sick, and trapped in this world's snares. We wrestle with life every day and need to hear from God to be able to discern what to do and how to do it. Anxiety will destroy us, and only the peace of God can guard the heart and mind.

The Word is God's message of love, provision, and protection, freely given to all who seek it. It strengthens faith and trust and helps to give a clear perspective of God's ability. Don't be content with yesterday's directions. With every new day, circumstances change, and just because you may have walked that way before does not mean the same response applies. Be renewed each day as you call upon Him; He will answer. God's Word is always fresh.

Seasons of Struggle

Therefore if any man be in Christ, he is a new creature; old
things are passed away, behold, all things are become new.
—2 Corinthians 5:17 (KJ)

Have you ever been through years of heartache and pain, in which your entire world seemed tossed upside down? Where you had family struggles, health challenges, and loss, all tearing at your heart? A cry goes out—if only the Lord hadn't allowed these things to happen. "*Why*, Lord?" During the dark days of the soul, your ability to respond rightly becomes warped in the darkness of isolation and fear.

How long can this go on? How long can we pray, when prayers appear to go unanswered? How long will friends and family endure our tales of woe before disappearing? Will others unselfishly sacrifice their time to encourage and pray for us when months become years?

Physical problems are real and require action as well as prayer. I addressed my physical needs each day, as I was able, but God carried me spiritually, for how could I have sustained my energy or sanity, if not through God's strength. When I was ill, I had limited energy. I remember praying, "One more minute, Lord. Just give me strength for one more minute." Some days I lived minute to minute. Being pulled in every direction at the same time is an impossible position to maintain without God's hands holding you together.

Whether you are the one going through the dark day of the soul, or you're the friend walking beside, great grace and faith are required. Remember that God knows your every thought, and whatever the enemy wants to use to harm you, God can use for the good. His ways are so much higher than ours, and His resolve is always right. Try to look past the circumstance, and focus on the one who has the power over circumstances. God wants to deliver us from the raw emotions that tear us apart.

I met a woman recently who, like me, had been fighting resentment. Both of our husbands had been through serious health issues, and both of us had our roles changed from wife to caregiver. She said she would drive down a lonely stretch of highway and just scream! Her anguish turned outward, but mine turned inward. Withdrawn, depressed, exhausted, resentful, and angry that my life was being stolen from me, I masked the pain to those around me. With so much consuming me and my time, I could hardly pray. I had to release my pain to two close friends and a prayer group. They prayed for me. I maintained professional behavior while working, but when I was alone, I suffered. I would sit in my bathtub and read Psalm 91, memorizing every word, which helped to drown out the voices screaming at me.

These were truly dark days, and only God knew when the season would pass. What then? I had crisis after crisis for seven years, and there was no end in sight. Would my husband be healed? What about my health, which was being sucked from me? Such a mix of emotions. On one hand, I knew I needed to care for the man I loved, but how was I to deal with everything? I had enough wisdom to know it wasn't my husband's fault, but I deeply resented heart disease. Could I ever become a wife again? I didn't know. My attitude had to change if I was to survive. I kept praying, and God, along with my two friends and prayer group, got me through. Don't discount the importance of spiritual friends. God places people around you to prevent you from isolation.

My role never fully changed back, but I did. I had entered an entirely new spiritual place.

So take heart, and hang in there. Victory is on the horizon. If God kept me from drowning in that storm-tossed ocean, He can do it for you too. God has promised to walk with you through those valleys, and He will *never* leave you. I know.

We are being changed from glory to glory, and our roots have had to grow deep to keep us from toppling over during the hailstorms of life. Walking through heart disease with my husband deepened my faith roots. Do I still battle resentment? Not that much anymore; it's fading. Through it all, God was faithful to hear and to answer the thousands of prayers that were prayed. Dick had a heart transplant in July 2011 and was home ten days later. God gave him his miracle.

I'm getting a picture of a tall skyscraper, towering over other buildings—a great structure. Its footings are deep to withstand the winds and possible earthquakes. I recently saw a documentary on the bullet train in China. Engineers poured footings twenty-three miles deep, to bedrock, over one stretch of track, stabilizing the track above. Both the skyscraper and the bullet train track were built with strong footings. Great man or woman of God, your footings are being poured deeper than you realize. Draw from the rivers of living water deep within you. They are there! Stand up and know that God is for you and not against you.

The Lord GOD hath given me the tongue of the learned, that
I should know how to speak a word in season to him that is
weary: he wakeneth morning by morning, he wakeneth mine
ear to hear as the learned. The Lord GOD hath opened mine
ear, and I was not rebellious, neither turned away back.
Isaiah 50:4–5 (KJV)
(Prophetic word about the Messiah)

O how love I thy law! It is my meditation all the day.
Thou through thy commandments hast made me wiser
than mine enemies: for they are ever with me. I have more
understanding than all my teachers: for thy testimonies
are my meditation. I understand more than the ancients,
because I keep thy precepts. I have refrained my feet
from every evil way, that I might keep thy word. I have
not departed from thy judgments: for thou hast taught
me. How sweet are thy words unto my taste! Yea, sweeter
than honey to my mouth! Through thy precepts I get
understanding: therefore I hate every false way. Thy word
is a lamp unto my feet, and a light unto my path.
Psalm 118:97–105 (KJV)
(Prophetic psalm about the Messiah)

Jesus loved God's law and meditated upon it all day, every day. God's
wisdom was far beyond that of His earthly teachers. Jesus knew more than
all those who surrounded Him, yet He remained humble, never departing
from His Father's instruction. The words of God were sweet to Him, and
their instruction gave Him understanding. God's voice was the lamp that
lit His path.

Think of the humility of Jesus, He, being God, knew infinitely more
than all those around him. *selah*

My father used to say, "If you can benefit from my mistakes, why wouldn't you take my advice and spare yourself?" Heeding advice from those far wiser than we, is prudent. Taking advice means submission—not deciding for yourself what is best but obeying another. My father had lived longer and had experienced so much more than I, so not taking his advice seemed foolish. What father, if his son asks for bread, would give him a stone? Or if he asks for a fish, would give him a snake? It was only logical to me to take my father's advice—he only wanted to spare me pain and hardship and bless me with positive results and success.

Jesus didn't need to learn, He was already wiser than any of his teachers, but because He was flesh and blood, He continually surrendered His fleshly desires to do His Father's will. Think about it. He obeyed and honored Mary and Joseph. *Selah.* He could have exercised His free will and allowed His soul and flesh to have their way, but then he would have fallen into the same trap as Adam. Instead, He released every word, thought, need, and desire of His soul, saying, "Not my will, but your will be done." Think of how submissive He was to Mary and Joseph. *Selah.* Think about God's submitting to human parents. What humility!

Morning after morning, Jesus arose to spend time with His Father. Jesus inclined His ears to listen to Him and then simply obeyed. Christ received the words that brought hope, and so can we. Take the Father's advice, and let God's perfect will flow through you. Receive the words that bring hope to the weary.

The Testimony

Then I heard a loud voice saying in heaven, "Now salvation, and
   strength, and the kingdom of our God, and the power of His
   Christ have come, for the accuser of our brethren, who accused
   them before our God day and night, has been cast down. And

they overcame him by the blood of the Lamb and by the word of
their testimony, and they did not love their lives to the death."
—Revelation 12:10–11 (NKJV)

There is power in the testimony. In our courts, testimonies determine the
fate of the accused. Many of our decisions are based upon the testimonies
of others. We eat at a restaurant or go on a vacation based on testimonies.
In advertising and news reporting—nearly everywhere we go—we are
inundated with testimonies. There is an assumption that testimonies are
true, but are they?

Testimonies aren't necessarily only spoken; many are unspoken.
Yesterday I was talking to a photographer on one of my projects, and the
subject of pro-life came up. I said that I was very pro-life, and his response
was, "Yes, I know." How did he know that? I don't even know his name.
We all read testimonies of how, throughout history, God's faithfulness has
existed. It is the awareness and understanding of God's faithfulness that
inspires us in our everyday walks. Scriptures and testimonies transform
those who read and hear them, but so can our testimonies.

In my opinion, the most effective counselor is the one who has walked
where I'm walking. Their testimonies carry enormous weight, and their
experience qualifies them by virtue of their experience. Our stories are ours
and cannot be disputed. It's highly unlikely that people seeking advice would
go to someone who had no understanding of the particular subject or prior
experience. Pastor and author Jon Courson writes, "Could it be that the
reason our sharing is sometime not received or effective is due to the fact that
we are speaking that which we ourselves have not touched, heard or seen?"

Interestingly enough, it is those hard life lessons that make our voices
credible, and it is in those hard places, lonely places, where God's presence is
evident. Always remember, Gods ways are not our ways, and His solutions
bring deliverance to the desperate.

The mother eagle pushes her babies out of the nest high on a cliff and
watches as they plummet toward the ground, again and again, until they
learn to fly. We too have been pushed out into the cruel world, again and
again, to learn how to catch the wind of the Spirit and fly. Be vulnerable.
Share your stories and the lessons God has taught you. I can't tell you the
number of times I have shared testimonies from my life and the salvations

and healing I've seen as a result. Nothing is without purpose. The difficult lessons have shaped you and can encourage and bring hope to others.

And even if our gospel is veiled, it is veiled to those who are perishing. The god of this age has blinded the minds of unbelievers, so that they cannot see the light of the gospel of the glory of Christ, who is the image of God.
—2 Corinthians 4:3–4 (NIV)

Satan, who is the god of this world, has blinded the minds of those who don't believe. They are unable to see the glorious light of the Good News. They don't understand this message about the glory of Christ, who is the exact likeness of God.
—2 Corinthians 4:3–4 (NLT)

The Word is very clear: people who have not received the grace of God are blind. We often shake our heads with disbelief at the worldly behavior of people around us, but human beings are living the only way they know. The unsaved live under Satan's deceptions and are veiled from the truth of the gospel.

A veil, according to *Webster's* is a concealing curtain or cover of cloth, something that hides or obscures. You cannot see what you cannot see, and you do not know what you do not know!

As a designer by trade, I often specify hardwood floors in my projects. After the wood is installed and cleaned, a rug is put into place, followed by furniture. The floor beneath that rug is concealed, veiled, and unless the furniture and the rug are removed, that floor will never be seen again.

Humans have been blinded by the realities of this world. Like the floor, all truth concerning the existence of an all-loving God is unseen.

If we are effective instruments, we are building relationships with those still living in darkness. Jesus said, "But when you give a banquet, invite the poor, the crippled, the lame, the blind, and you will be blessed. Although they cannot repay you, you will be repaid at the resurrection of the righteous. In short. Jesus is saying to build relationships with the lost, the wounded, and those unable to walk on their own, and you will be blessed.

Have you ever wondered why so many believers work in the marketplace? The world is full of people who are lost, lame, crippled, and blind—the very ones Jesus told us to invite to the banquet. God has actually put you in the marketplace for a reason, and if you build genuine, loving relationships with those you live by or work around, resistant barriers will come down. As you bless and love your family and friends, they will open themselves to you. People are prone to believe what you say, once they know you care.

Pray that God will use you to build true relationships, and watch love do its work. Unless the veil is lifted from our eyes, we will not go any deeper. We must be transformed in our hearts and minds and allow God to unveil false perceptions and false motives in our own lives. Let's free ourselves from the bondage of religious techniques and allow the Holy Spirit to move through us to labor with Christ in His work here on earth.

Thy Kingdom Come

Thy kingdom come, Thy will be done on earth, as it is in heaven.
—Matthew 6:10 (KJV)

Be not wise in thine own eyes: fear the LORD, and depart from evil. It shall be health to thy navel, and marrow to thy bones.
—Proverbs 3:7–8 (KJV)

Be of the same mind one toward another. Mind not high things, but condescend to men of low estate. Be not wise in your own conceits.
—Romans 12:16 (KJV)

"Thy kingdom come" was spoken out of the mouth of God. The Creator Emmanuel, God with us, has spoken; it will happen. His kingdom come, His will be done on earth as it is in heaven.

So don't be wise in your own eyes, but fear the Lord and abstain from every worldly way. Just like the navel is the means by which a mother supplies nourishing life to the child within her womb, and just as marrow supplies necessary nourishing moisture to healthy bones, fearing God and abstaining from evil brings nourishing life to each child of God, if we are living as God Himself showed us to live.

When you were a child, you spoke like a child and acted like a child, but when you became an adult, you put away childish things. When you were lost in your sin, deceived and blinded by this world, you sounded like the world and operated in worldly ways, but when you were saved, did you put away your worldly garment?

You are connected to God by a lifeline that supplies your every need. God's kingdom culture provides protection and provision, and you have been set apart for kingdom purposes. Are you being used as a vehicle for God's will to be effectively achieved? Maybe it's time to say no to the world and stop striving for high and lofty things. Humble yourself, and allow God's grace to facilitate every day of your life. Let His creative words, His amazing love, His great grace, His incredible mercy, His flawless wisdom, and His human humility flow through you, advancing His kingdom day by day and moment by moment.

> Giving all diligence, add to your faith virtue, to virtue
> knowledge, to knowledge self-control, to self-control
> perseverance, to perseverance godliness, to godliness
> brotherly kindness, and to brotherly kindness love.
> —2 Peter 1:5–7 (KJ)

The Bible says we who are born again have been given a divine nature so that we can lead godly lives. Our thinking and behavior should align with this new nature, but at times we revert back to our old selves. We all have had days fall apart, but it is what we do *on those days* that speaks. Will we show mercy? Will we be patient? Will we be kind? Will we control ourselves and do what is right in God's eyes? If someone hurts our feelings, will we forgive? It is our choice.

Peter is writing instructions for godly living, and although God's grace covers us, Peter reminds us of our responsibility to cultivate our own Christian growth. Is your heart yielded to God? Do you want to follow the Lord in all of your ways? As humans, we will all fall short because we live in a chaotic, fallen world, but if your heart seeks the high road, the Lord will give you the strength to resist anger, temptations, discouragement, gossip, unforgiveness, and so forth, because He always helps a yielded heart. There always will be frustrations, and Christians need to cooperate with God and confidently approach life's challenges. Spirituality is a choice; it does not come automatically.

Pray you will be able to resist that old nature with the help of the Holy Spirit, and fight the good fight. Abstain from fleshly lures that attack your soul. Your old nature pulls you back into your old behaviors, so daily work out your salvation. God will provide the strength when you are weak. He will make a way where there seems to be no way. Trust Him to help you, and call on the Holy Spirit to give you what you need. His mercies are new every morning. Believe it, trust it, and work at it with all of your heart. Exercise your spiritual muscles by purposefully showing kindness, smiling, being helpful, showing grace, and being merciful. The blessings you will receive far outweigh old behaviors. Do what is right in God's eyes, not necessarily yours. He is faithful if we are.

Therefore, my dear friends, as you have always obeyed—not
only in my presence, but now much more in my absence—
continue to *work out your salvation* with fear and trembling"
(Philippians 2:12, emphasis added)

Washed Clean

Then the angel showed me Joshua the high priest standing
before the angel of the Lord. The Accuser, Satan,_was
there at the angel's right hand, making accusations against
Joshua. And the Lord said to Satan, "I, the Lord, reject
your accusations, Satan. Yes, the Lord, who has chosen
Jerusalem, rebukes you. This man is like a burning stick
that has been snatched from the fire." Joshua's clothing
was filthy as he stood there before the angel. So the angel
said to the others standing there, "Take off his filthy
clothes." And turning to Joshua he said, "See, I have taken
away your sins, and now I am giving you these fine new
clothes." Then I said, "They should also place a clean
turban on his head." So they put a clean priestly turban on
his head and dressed him in new clothes while the angel
of the Lord stood by. Zechariah 3:1–5 (NLT)

...For the one who accuses our brothers, who
accuses them day and night ...
—Revelation 12:10 (NIV)

Our enemy, the devil, constantly accuses us, day and night. We hear his
accusations and too often live in fear and shame, believing the twisted

realities of our pasts. Scripture is clear; we all have sinned and fall short of the glory of God, and too often, we, when faced with our pasts, revert back to our old human nature. Learn to recognize when you are laboring with the devil and falling into your old life without hope, or remembering the work of the cross. Jesus has wiped away all of our past wrongs, and we are free from that dark world, so instead of hiding in shame, hopelessness, or self-pity, give it to God, and leave it there. You can never undo what has been done, but you can learn and move forward. God alone has the power to heal the scars and use it for good.

For believers, confronting our sinful nature honestly is a conscious decision; take off the old and put on the new. Somewhere in our past, we all *were* hopelessly lost and blind to the depth of our own depravity; we *were* consumed with satisfying our selfish nature and with controlling our own destinies. Remembering those days is one thing; lingering in them is another. While it is easier to do what we have always done, the Lord wants us to live differently.

All your past behavioral patterns are stored deep in your subconscious, and living as a new creation in Christ goes against those natural instinctual behaviors. To live with an entirely different perspective, apart from the old worldviews of the past, takes work, so study the Word, and ask the Holy Spirit to help you. Keep your mind fixed upon Jesus, and memorize the promises of God so that you may become alive to the divine nature and escape this world's corruption and its evil desires. Practice adding to your faith goodness, knowledge, self-control, perseverance, godliness, kindness, and love. Possessing these qualities in increasing measure will keep you from being ineffective and unproductive in your war against the old nature. Resist going backward, and lean upon the Holy Spirit to help you daily. Our enemy, Satan, is defeated, and if God is for you, who can stand against you?

> Therefore, my dear friends, as you have always obeyed—
> not only in my presence, but now much more in my
> absence—continue to *work out* your *salvation* with
> fear and trembling.
> —Philippians 2:12 (NIV)

When you look at Jesus, you might observe that nothing, by this world's standards, fits the "normal" description of a king. He was born of a virgin, raised by a lowly couple in an impoverished little town, and had a questionable origin. Mary and Joseph still had to pay taxes and live with the scorn of their neighbors. Jesus had to work. He wore no crown and died a criminal's death. His life is directly opposite of our view of royalty.

We have been brainwashed to believe in this world's systems and have been living accordingly. This type of mind-set contradicts the principles of God's kingdom. Submission to Christ, righteous living, and pure motives transform worldly believers into kingdom dwellers. The kingdom of this world is corrupt, but Jesus overcame by yielding His human will to do His Father's will. So too must we, moment by moment, work out our salvation, redeeming our minds, wills, and emotions.

In this world, people go through life looking for help but finding little. Is the government the answer? What about a job? The expression "dog-eat-dog world" describes a ruthless competitive environment, and to the victor go the spoils. That is the world we live in. But there is a different world, where help is available, where we are loved, and everlasting peace is given. When love and help are available, why would anyone desire to strain and struggle on his or her own? We, who love the Lord and want to live within His kingdom, have to consciously work at redeeming our minds. Let's make righteous decisions and follow Christ, not our emotions.

I remember using Mother's washboard as a little girl. Mom always had me scrub Dad's shirt collar with Lava soap before putting it into the washing machine. There are years of "stinkin' thinkin'" in all of us, and we too need to scrub our minds from wrongful thinking.

Paul says to work out your salvation. He doesn't say work *for* your salvation or work *on* your salvation but work out your salvation—and working out equates to exercise. Living the way Jesus instructed us to live is very difficult until it becomes habit. While change may be hard at first, it will set you free. You don't have to be angry or vengeful; you can have joy and be forgiving. What is God calling you to work out—a bad habit, an unforgiving heart, a resentful spirit, negative thinking, lack of trust, a secret craving, a grudge, hard feelings, a poverty mind-set, or a controlling, manipulative issue?

Jesus had many hurdles to overcome before taking His kingly throne. We don't often think of Christ as a man, but he had many of the same issues as we have. He had to resist temptations and exercise discipline. Can you imagine Jesus as a child—the maturity and restraint it took not to be like the other children? I wonder if the townsfolk ever moved past His mysterious birth. Think about how easy it would have been to snub or harbor anger toward those who looked down on His mom. It must have been difficult for Christ the man not to retaliate against those stripping, spitting on, and nailing him to the cross. Think about how extraordinary He was as a man. *Selah.* He should always be our role model.

Note: "There is controversy over the criminal charges that were used to justify Jesus' crucifixion. Ultimately, at His trial Jesus was asked by Pontius Pilate if He was a king. Though He denied ruling an earthly kingdom, the Roman legal system branded Him a traitor, guilty of treason. His was a capital offense with a penalty of crucifixion" (David J. Shestokas, "The Criminal Penalty of Crucifixion," March 5, 2013, Published by Constitutional Sound Bites).

Your Job

> "Do you not say, 'There are yet four months, and then
> comes the harvest'? Behold, I say to you, lift up your eyes
> and look on the fields, that they are white for harvest."
> —John 4:35 (NASB)

When I began my business over forty years ago, there weren't books or seminars about bringing Christianity into the workplace. It was the Lord's and the Holy Spirit's faithful leading that kept me on track, and it was they who opened doors for me to know other on-fire Christians who, like me, worked outside the church.

There are three very different categories of marketplace believers: (1) people who truly enjoy their jobs and have no desire to go into any kind of ministry; (2) marketplace people who want to get out of business and go into full-time congregational ministry; and (3) those who enjoy business and are fully aware that their work is their ministry.

Everyone eventually finds a profession that interests them. Once employed, individuals begin to work in that field with hopeful intentions of success. This first group spends most of their lives developing skills and establishing themselves in their professions. God does not seem to play much of a role in their everyday work life. They still believe in Jesus and go to church on Sunday, but the rest of the week belongs to work.

Those in the second group see beyond the physical reality of work and see God moving in their day-to-day lives. They want to involve Him in every aspect of their lives but don't know how to mix Christianity and business. They feel like Lone Rangers and find little satisfaction in their work. This group truly does not see their work as ministry, and because they see their Christian lives as somewhat fruitless, they either live with the frustration or quit their jobs to go to seminary. God may be calling some of them into full-time ministry, but a great majority of these were designed for the marketplace. They simply can't see it.

Those in the third group are confident in what they are doing. They actually see their work as their ministry and are aware that God is using them right where they are. They have jumped over the religious roadblocks, spiritual prototypes, and normal business practices to discover their purpose outside the congregational walls. The harvest fields are very visible, and they see the necessity of staying in the world where they can be the most effective. This is the ultimate destination for workplace Christians. The challenge lies in remaining in the marketplace where they can be effectively used without becoming annoyingly religious. Jesus said that He was leaving us here not to be of the world but to live in the world.

Marketplace ministry is hard work for this third group because they often don't see immediate fruit for their spiritual labors. Fighting worldliness and remaining virtuous every day is tough, but the daily opportunity to love, serve, and pray for people is an awesome privilege, and each day is filled with divine appointments. Being a Christ-centered ambassador in the world takes mature believers who fully lean on their close-knit relationship with Christ.

I find it interesting that for over forty years, God has been teaching and showing me the importance of marketplace ministry. Although it has been difficult to stay in the business world, God has held me fast and has never let me leave it. In looking back, I see it is where I belonged. My frustrations ceased when I finally relinquished my need to be used inside the church and simply trusted God. "Whatever you do, do your work heartily, as for the Lord rather than for men" (Colossians 3:23). God can and does use you. We are the laborers, so go out into the harvest fields, and serve the Lord in whatever you do.

Your Mind-Set

> For as he thinks in his heart, so is he.
> —Proverbs 23:7 (NKJV)

Where is that place where freedom abides, the place where darkness is dispelled and God is glorified? How do we get there?

It has been my observation over the years that freedom or bondage is in the mind. Life's circumstances dictate our attitudes, if we let them, but God has given believers the free will to choose how we respond to any given circumstance. Before receiving Christ, our eyes were veiled, and we were bound to the lies and deceptions of the devil, but at the moment we believed upon the Lord Jesus Christ, we were set free to trust God's Word and act in faith. Eleanor Roosevelt once said, "No one can make you feel inferior without your consent." Someone once said to me, "No one can make you sad." Low self-esteem or sadness can only cripple us if we receive it. What you allow into your mind determines your mind-set.

Every event throughout your life is locked into your mind. Good or bad, these experiences are hidden deep within your subconscious. Throughout the day you react to stimuli, words, and events. The stimuli will first go to your subconscious mind, which will trigger an immediate response before your conscious mind can make a deliberate decision. The subconscious mind is your belief center; it is what you believe. To say it again, it is in the subconscious where your deeply planted beliefs lie. If you have lived in an environment where you have had little support or love, your instantaneous reactions will be entirely different from someone who has been raised around love. We all have been raised in a fallen world, and everything in our subconscious minds is already established. Obviously not all is bad, but some of our beliefs are. Christ has bought your freedom, and He is the only one who can deliver the wrong beliefs from your mind. Ask Him to identify those areas that are alien to God's Word. Pray for deliverance and work daily in those areas to combat the inner lies. Memorize scripture that pertains to your issue, and speak those verses out loud to yourself. (Faith comes by hearing.) For example, most of us have self-identity issues. God says we are His finest masterpiece. *Do you believe you are fearfully and wonderfully made?* (Psalm139:14). Are you going to believe what God says or what your mind tells you?

We are in a spiritual war zone for our minds, caught in between heaven and hell. Our enemy's aim is to steal, kill, and destroy. If his lies can deceive us into thinking anything other than what God says about us, he has succeeded. I have seen passionate believers retreat when the battle gets too hard. For sure, life will be easier when passion is squelched, but God said in His Word to fight the good fight and to keep standing. War is not easy, and there will be casualties, but God says, "Do not throw away your confidence", God is able to deliver and heal your mind. "You need to persevere so when you have done the will of God, you will receive what He has promised." (Hebrews 10:35-36 NIV)

CONCLUSION

"Because he loves me," says the Lord, "I will rescue him; I will
protect him, for he acknowledges my name. He will call on
me, and I will answer him; I will be with him in trouble, I will
deliver him and honor him. With long life I will satisfy him
and show him my salvation."
—Psalm 91:14–16 (NIV)

Psalm 91:14-16 was read at my father's funeral. It's one of my favorites
and has been engraved upon my heart. Over these past fourteen years, I
have had to learn how to trust. The Word says, "Do not be anxious about
anything, but in every situation, pray with thanksgiving, and God will give
you peace." (Philippians 4:6) I believe when trust is present, peace becomes
an invisible shield that surrounds me—it's like being in the eye of a storm.
When there is no way I can stand and without knowing which way to go;
when circumstances look as if I will surely drown, my flesh screams panic.
But God says, "Be still and know that I am God." That stillness is a deep
trust, a supernatural gift, acquired, I believe, only through fire.

Once the Lord showed me that the kingdom of God is like floating in
the ocean. We must trust Him to keep us afloat and trust His Holy Spirit
to blow us where He wants us to go. The trust that has emerged from my
life's history with God keeps me floating.

Trust in the LORD with all your heart and
lean not on your own understanding.
—Proverbs 3:5 (NIV)

Printed in the United States
By Bookmasters